WHEE
MOUNTAIN

── THE ──
HIGH PEAK
TRAIL

Tim Woodcock

future
BOOKS

Dedication

For Kay, John and Chris

First published in 1995 by

Future Books

a division of Future Publishing Limited
Beauford Court, 30 Monmouth Street, Bath BA1 2BW

Typeset and designed by D & N Publishing, Ramsbury, Wiltshire

Cover design by Maria Bowers

A CIP catalogue record for this book is available from the British Library

ISBN: 1 85981 0950

Printed and bound by BPC Paulton Books Ltd.
A member of the British Printing Company

2 4 6 8 10 9 7 5 3 1

If you would like more information on our other cycling titles please write to:
The Publisher, Future Books at the above address

CONTENTS

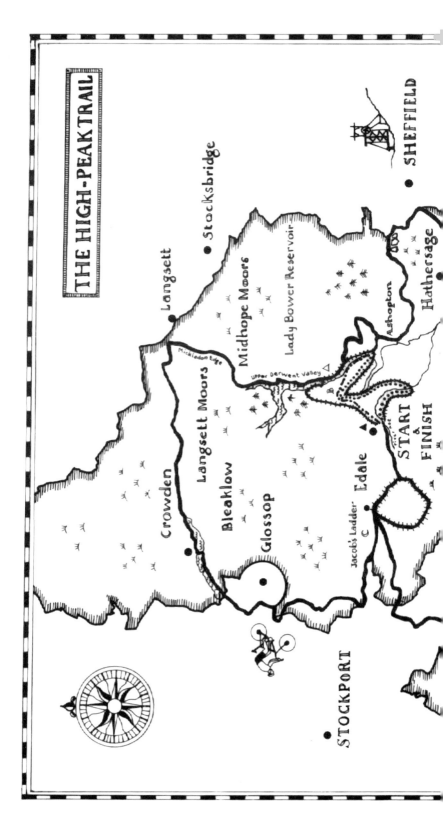

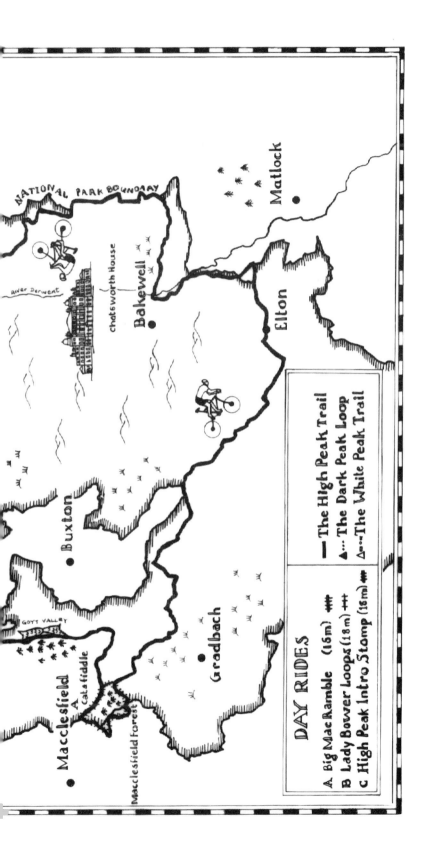

DAY RIDES

A Big Mac Ramble (15m)
B Lady Bower Loops (18m)
C High Peak Intro Stomp (15m)

— The High Peak Trail
▲··· The Dark Peak Loop
△··· The White Peak Trail

Foreword

It is the job of the National Park authorities to protect and enhance unique landscapes and to provide recreational opportunities for the millions of people who visit them every year. The Peak became the first British National Park in 1951, and in many respects, it was a National Park where it was most needed. Completely surrounded by the great industrial cities of the north and Midlands, the Peak District was a last green and unspoilt island at the southern end of the Pennines.

The Park covers 555 square miles (1,438 sq. km) and parts of six different counties. There are two Peak Districts; the White Peak in the centre and south, where pearly-grey limestone breaks the surface; and the Dark Peak, where sombre millstone grit forms the underlying rock of the high moorlands in the north and to the east and west. Each area has its special character; and many visitors enjoy the softer, settled landscape of the White Peak where a network of drystone walls covers a rolling plateau split by steep-sided dales. In contrast, the Dark Peak has fewer signs of humanity, and the bleak, peat and heather covered moors are the domain of hardy creatures like the red grouse and mountain hare. The moors are fringed by the famous Peak District 'edges' which frown down on lush shale river valleys.

Part of The High Peak Trail links up with the National Park's own High Peak Trail railpath, where former railway lines provide the rider with fine, scenic routes through the limestone countryside of the White Peak. The railpath trails provide a sanctuary for wild flowers. Some sections are now designated as Nature Reserves by the Derbyshire Wildlife Trust. Plants such as the blue meadow cranesbill and harebell can be seen, while lapwings (pee-wits) regularly flock here in Spring.

Responsible use of the Park is encouraged at all times. Included in this book are 'off-road codes', equipping the rider with a code of conduct for exploring the area with care and consideration for the Park's outstanding natural beauty.

Peak District National Park Authority

Descending into Edale down the delightful Hollins Cross track.

INTRODUCTION

The Ride

Not more than a dozen miles from the centre of Sheffield you can be snaking down skittish single-track, pitting your skills against a severe landscape where solitude and isolation still reign supreme. Or spinning down a greenway, short-cropped turf cushioning your progress and your horizons hemmed in by the craggy cliffs of a limestone gorge. This is the High Peak Trail. Six days of superlative off-roading in the Peak District that encapsulates everything that's great about mountain biking in Britain. And all contained within a 165 mile loop that circumnavigates the 500 square mile National Park.

The first National Park to be created, the Peak District is an upland gem hanging off the southern tip of the Pennine Chain. No National Park has a richer tapestry on which we can ride. From the delightful, thyme-scented Long Dale in the south to the grim, wind-swept Howden Moors of the north the landscape of the Peak is full of contrasts. Contrasts that reflect the rock on which it's set: pale limestone in the south, drab gritstone to the north. The White and Dark Peak. Landscapes in opposition, their variety is the key to the fascination that riding the High Peak Trail never fails to provide.

The Rider

After completing the Trail Chris Marley, a vet cross-country racer of national standing, described the ride in one word 'Stunning!' then added 'This is serious mountain biking territory.' But he wasn't just commenting on the scenery – stunning as it is – he was stunned by the sheer power needed to cope with the climbs and the technical twists that the High Peak Trail threw in his path. But don't be put off. OK, so Chris is an accomplished rider, but I'm not. The word 'pootle' springs to mind when I spin the cranks and, though I found bits on the limits of bikeable, I rose to each off-road challenge – some conquered, some not – and came away from Edale a far better biker than the one that arrived.

The Route

The High Peak Trail is really the marriage of two, separate rides – the White Peak Loop and the Dark Peak Loop – where the resulting union is greater than the sum of the two parts. That's because the marriage is made in the Vale of Edale where the interleaving gritstone and limestone has left a legacy of exceptional off-roading to be enjoyed.

It's a legendary mountain bike landscape full of famous names: Jacobs Ladder, Stanage Edge, Cave Dale, Winnats Pass, The Roych, Mickelden Edge... These are just a few of the places featured in the routes contained within this book together with new off-road trails never before published. And there are routes to suit whatever time window you've got available to slip in some superb cycling. It is, however, advisable to study the routes carefully, to ensure your fitness ability is compatible with the more demanding stretches of terrain.

To begin with there's always the full, mountain bike experience; six to seven days cycling the 165 mile High Peak Trail. Or if you want a short, sharp challenge then take a long weekend and tackle the 60 mile Dark Peak Loop; if you like a longer, slightly less radical ride the White Peak Loop, a four to five day jaunt covering 125 miles of very mixed terrain might well suit. The link to the Dark Peak offers the rider an alternative outbound route from the starting point at Edale YHA, which joins the main route at Ladybower Reservoir.

Alternatively, the link from the White Peak Loop provides a shorter and more gentle home-bound route, which connects the Trail on Day 5 at Ladybower Reservoir with Edale. But if this sounds all too much, and you can only spare the odd day, you can split the Trail into day-size bites or take time out to enjoy one of the three day loops.

Tim Woodcock
1995

BEFORE YOU GO

Off-road routes in the Peak are characterised by their technical edge.
Not the white-knuckle, put a step wrong and you're dead technical but
an edge that demands absolute concentration. Relax for an instant
during an ascent and grip will slip, you'll dab, stop, and getting re-
started can be nigh on impossible. Often it's just your sheer
determination plus a degree of dexterity with power delivery that will
get you through. And that takes fitness.

But being fit is not just a question of power. It's more about recovery
rate and in the Peaks there's little let-up in the roller-coaster regime.
Legs that are quick to revive are not just an asset but a necessity. Being
in shape to take a mountain bike off-road in a landscape as rugged as
this is difficult to pick up on the trail. That's because fitness gains are
made during the period of rest between spells of activity. No rest and
no fitness gain. So you can't really pick it up in the few days before you
go either.

The ideal time to think about getting trim is ten weeks or so before
the departure date. I know it's a long time, puts paid to travelling on a
whim and the word 'preparation' rears its ugly head, but being fit will
make the whole escapade more fun. For everyone. Even MTBers who
get out and hit the hills regularly will benefit from some serious
working out on their wheels. By the time you set off from Edale you
ought to have a few thirty mile day loops under your belt; otherwise
you'll need to slot in a couple of days furlough to allow that extra
fitness to build.

Rides like this are an enriched experience if you're in good company.
A well-integrated team is much better able to overcome adversities with
ease; even if it's a simple thing like bad weather. But travelling
companions are notoriously tricky to choose and in the ups and downs
betwixt the beginning and the end there will be stresses and strains.
Long distance off-roading is not all fun. On precipitous trails it's both
difficult and demanding; add fatigue, perhaps a mis-read map and a
ferocious wind and you've got a pretty good recipe for a falling out.
Always distressing, discord can soon develop into dispute and that
could be dangerous in the wrong place at the wrong time. Choose
companions carefully. It goes without saying that you should all get on

Rushup Edge has some superb, semi-technical track that'll keep your trail skills up to scratch and etch a grin on your face.

but don't forget fitness. One mismatch – couch potato or fitness freak – in an otherwise well balanced band of bikers will often lead to persistent friction and cast a shadow over the whole party.

Kitting Out

HARDWARE

Travel light and ride free. Whatever you've got, you've got to carry it on this trip. And when you're making height-gains in excess of 3000ft on most days, you'll appreciate that trimming kit to a necessary minimum makes sense. Providing you don't overdo it and skimp on essentials, saving weight is safer too. It conserves energy and makes handling a bike on some of the more extreme terrain a lot less hairy. Heavy bikes tend to keep going when they get kicked off course!

The Wheels

I could launch into a diatribe about how terrific titanium is, that suspension is for sissies and how SPDs are essential for smooth power transfer. Then tell you how to mortgage the house to finance the purchasing of that 'must have everything trick' type frameset. But I won't. To begin with bike choice is a personal thing, fads and fashions change on a whim and providing it's sound any clunker of an MTB will do. Having said that, there are some pointers as to what makes a bike well suited to the task and what does not.

You're going to travel some steep and technical trails so use a good quality, reasonably light, proper MTB – 21 or more indexed gears – with alloy wheels, low gearing, pannier rack braze-ons and a comfortable saddle. We're talking several hundred pounds here, but if you're serious about mountain biking it's worth it. Take a look at the mountain biking press for what's what then ask at a good mountain bike shop and buy the best that you can afford. If that's out of your budget then consider hiring one. Hiring is also a good way of 'balancing out' the hardware within your group. This is especially important if, for example, one of you has a clunker and the rest are riding lightweight titanium trickery decked out with suspension. On a long distance ride the difference in ride quality will be amplified, perhaps to the extent that it'll put a downer on the whole trip. Your bike should also be thoroughly serviced and checked out before setting off. A wheel buckle might well bring an early end to your long awaited trip but a collapse could spell disaster, so have your wheels trued before you start.

Some bike accessories that should be considered essential are: bottle cages – back-pack drink carriers and rucksacks don't always work well together – a brand new set of the best brake blocks you can afford and some branded, good quality treads, with around a 2in carcass of new rubber for cushioning and grip. Consult a good MTB bike shop for what's the latest trend in tyres and avoid cheap 'imitations'; they're usually made with low-grade compound and won't grip so well. On this ride there's also a case for some sort of cushioning up front, to negate the effects of day-on-day riding the rough stuff. Proper suspension is ideal but one of the many forms of 'flex-stem' will also fend off fatigue.

Other items to consider, especially if long distance off-roading really grabs you, are: an A headset or a headset lock-ring, Allen-key crank fittings such as Crank-o-Matics, a bomb-proof set of wheels, puncture-proof tubes and a sprung saddle or suspension seat post. If you have SPDs check that your shoes have a deep, aggressive tread. If they don't, then seriously consider re-fitting your old pedals and clips and wear walking boots instead. The loss in power transfer will be minimal and they'll offer a much firmer footing when it comes to shouldering the frameset. Especially over grass. Some SPDs also suffer from clogging when it gets really gloopy. And it can get seriously gloopy on the southern White Peak Loop!

I fitted, but never used, a pannier rack on this trip as the tracks were mostly so rocky that there were few occasions when a pack could be safely strapped to it. Having said that, there's a fair amount of tarmac, pannier racks are the next best thing to a mudguard (another item that's worth it's weight in gold), and you might be glad to give your back a rest once in a while. Whatever you do, buy a top quality rack – cheap ones will collapse under the constant stress of trail-shock – and preferably a hollow-tubed, chromoly one.

Tools and Spares

Quality doesn't come cheap but good tools are a godsend when you're in a fix, so be prepared to pay for them. Most multi-tools will save weight on a tool-roll of separate bits, but don't forget to check that your clever widget does all the whatsits on your bike. And your companions'.

The same goes for spares. If you all run the same tyre valves, chains, straddle wires and even brake blocks the stores can be kept to a sensible size. Once you've got all tools and spares together, pack them tight and keep them handy – ready for the inevitable trail-side emergency. The High Peak Trail does take you through some pretty bleak and isolated scenery; even so, there's no need to go over the top with the wilderness thing and go carrying enough spares for a total re-build. There's a major population centre within a dozen miles of you most of the time.

SOFTWARE

We're all aware of the weather's profound effect on our well-being – in the wet it's doom and gloom but once the sun pops out life's a party. Clothing's like that. Except clothing choice is not dictated on a whim of Nature. Kit yourself out with inappropriate gear that's been moth-balled in the wardrobe for the past five years and you're dressing up for a dose of doom and gloom. Uncomfortable. But take some time in selecting good quality kit and you'll be pleased to face whatever the weather throws at you.

Even in summer controlling warmth is the vital element, versatility the name of the game. Up on the Pennine ridge it's a lot colder than down amongst the urban sprawl that surrounds the Peak District.

Dress Sense

Kitting out a mountain biker has proved to be the outdoor clothes designers' biggest challenge yet. It's a strenuous sport that generates loads of heat at peak activity, then the loonies stand about mending punctures on a hillside with a wind-chill factor of -10°C and their body temperature drops like the proverbial stone. But designers are rising to the challenge and there's a stack of really good, MTB-specific gear to choose from.

The multi-layer principle is bandied about as the way to go – and it works – but there's always someone who has to swim against the tide and now there're one or two manufacturers producing single-layer, pile-lined kit but it's really late season/winter wear and ideal for weight-saving freaks. So right from the start we're faced with a bewildering choice of kit, complicated by contrasting design convictions and all so technical that you need a science degree to discern what's what. The best approach is to decide what you want the clothing to do. For long trips it has to be light, have low bulk, be quick drying, resist the rampant sock syndrome, be easy to care for, fit well, feel comfortable and perform well. Whether it's to wick, provide warmth, windproofing or water resistance. (You'll need clothing to perform all of these functions.) Above all it has to let your body lose moisture and 'breathe'. Under-layer clothing that soaks up water

Ramsley Wood where gravity-suck and scenery vie for your attention.

and sags like a wet flannel are useless. Likewise a top-layer that's built like a tent, flies like a kite and gives you your very own greenhouse effect is best left at home. MTB magazines regularly review kit, back-issues are easily obtainable and their advice should put you on the right track.

Comfort après-trail is fundamental to your well-being. You'll want to have a shower and step into some light longs, slip on a T and put those trail-weary toes into a pair of pliable shoes. Pack-down bulk and weight is especially important with après-trail togs – they'll be on your back most of the time.

On your feet there's nothing to beat a good pair of MTB boots. That's boots, not shoes. Alternatives such as light walking boots and even fell-running shoes with modified soles grip well and give ankle support. Don't be tempted by making do with trainers unless you're good at grass skiing with a bike on your back. Even a modest grass bank can become insurmountable if your boots sport an inadequate sole. Last, but definitely not least, wear a helmet!

Navigation Aids
Well you can dispense with the bulky package of maps that's the bane of most long distance rides. They're in the back of this book. Add to that a good quality compass on a neck cord and weather-proof cycle computer – both of which you must be able to use with ease – and that's the pilot part sorted.

Health and Survival Gear
Mountain biking can be dangerous; a trivial accident up at Edale Cross or a major fall along Mickelden Edge can quickly bring you down to a survival situation. A matter of life or death. Given the right kit, make the right decisions and you can turn crisis to drama, live to tell the tale and even laugh about it. Later. A good first aid kit and the knowledge

to use it are essential. A basic kit should include anti-sceptic wipes, plasters, cohesive tape for wounds, triangular bandage, salt tablets for cramp, Puritabs and first aid instructions. (First aid information, covering some of the common MTB emergencies, is given on pages 25–7). Whoever comes to your aid might not be an accomplished first-aider and they, not to mention you, will appreciate a set of instructions ready to hand. Survival gear – mini torch, survival bag and whistle – can all be packed with the first aid kit. Pack it in a heavy-duty, zip-tie polythene bag, label it clearly and know where it is.

Not strictly first aid but pretty important to the health department are medicaments for treating minor ailments like saddle soreness (not minor if it happens, but Sudacream or E45 cream speed recovery), athlete's foot, sun burn, lip chaff, muscle strain and pain.

Other Stuff

Mountain biking's a dirty business, so the personal hygiene department needs careful thought. Apart from the usual salves and unguents for bodily application some micro wash liquid is a good idea to keep those shorts clean and fresh on a day-to-day basis. Remember too that you'll need a small, quick drying towel.

In the Bag

Fell walkers will be a common sight on parts of the trail and many of them will be using pint-sized day-packs to take their kit. Take a leaf out of their book. Travel light and leave it on your back.

A small rucksack – about 30l capacity – together with either a bumbag or a small barbag should be fine. Features to look for are a narrow profile, light weight, waist and chest security straps, wide shoulder straps (easily adjusted and locked), compression straps and a low pack height. (Try it out, packed full, with your helmet on. Look straight up and if the helmet is knocked forwards over your eyes, then that's what will happen on the bike.) Such features can often be found on climbing and fell-running backpacks but there are MTB-specific rucksacks that can be swopped from back to a pannier rack and back with ease.

If you have problems packing all your kit, roll the clothes into tight cylinders, and tie them with compression straps (Velcro straps are ideal). Remember to put the least dense gear at the bottom, the heaviest at the top and ensure the back-panel is comfortable against your spine.

High Peak Trail Kit List

A handy, pre-'flight' check list is provided but don't regard it as defin-
itive. Lists are an important aid to successful trip planning – a finely
honed trip-list is one of the most valuable bits of kit you'll ever use –
and making your own will encourage you to evaluate each item on its
merits. Try the one below for starters.

If you're expecting cold, wet weather you'll need to add extra clothing,
especially thermals (tights, tops and socks), full gloves, headband/snood
and waterproof socks. On the hardware side don't forget lights – you
may be caught out in the dark.

How heavy will this lot weigh? For a summer circuit aim for about
12-14lbs for all your personal kit and about 7lbs of shared gear
(including food).

TOOL KIT
Pump
Tyre levers
Full set of Allen keys
Small, adjustable wrench
Screwdriver (cross-head
and flat)
Chain-splitter
Spoke key
Penknife

BIKE SPARES
Inner tube
Puncture repair kit
Brake blocks
Straddle wire
Lube
Rear gear cable
Rear light/batteries
Cable ties
Allen bolts for bottle
cages, etc.
Gaffer/carpet tape
Couple of spare chain
links
Cable lock
Water bottle(s)

CYCLE CLOTHING
Padded shorts
(2 pairs min.)
Sports socks
(3 pairs min.)
Cool shirt, short-sleeved
Cycle shirt, long-sleeved
Wicking/thermal top
Bike mitts
Helmet
(not extreme, elongated,
aero-type)
Fleece/mid-layer top
Windproof top
Waterproof top with
hood
Tights or windproof
over-trousers
MTB Boots

APRÈS TRAIL
Light-weight longs
Underwear
Shorts
Baseball boots/sandals or
similar

PERSONAL KIT
Wash kit inc. towel
Zipped wallet with
money
Plastic
YHA card/B&B contacts
Pencil
Sewing kit (polyester
thread)
Medical kit
Head torch/batteries

TRAIL KIT
Compass
Computer
First aid kit
Survival kit
(whistle, bag, torch)
Emergency food
(cereal bars, etc.)
Rucksack with liner
Bar/bum bag (to keep em-
ergency kit separated)

Accommodation

From the first one of the key considerations is where you are going to sleep. Even how you are going to sleep. Comfort and a good night's rest are keynotes to the success of long distance cycling and only you will know what your absolute needs are. Consider them carefully – you owe it to yourself.

Camping

Camping and self-sufficiency seem to go hand-in-hand with the adventure of mountain biking but – and it's a big but – the penalties are high. Tent, stove, sleeping bag, mat, cooking kit and food plus additional clothes and the outsized rucksack to put it all in will weigh you down by an extra stone or so and can make technical trail riding ridiculously difficult. Descents are interesting though, if lethal! Survivors, exhausted by a day beneath their burden, will then have the pleasure of finding a pitch, setting the tent, searching out a stream, fetching the water and washing cold. Then it's cook, eat, clean-up and finally fall into a stupor only to be driven spare at the crack of dawn by a demented bunch of birds doing their dawn chorus thing!

Camping's great. Then there's the very real problem of security. The big city is never very far away and the Peaks suffer from a perennial theft problem.

Bed and Breakfast

By way of comparison, at the opposite extreme, we have B&Bs. First and foremost you can dump all that camping kit and ride light. Not day-ride light but nimble enough to loft wheels, bunny hop and skip the rear end round the odd rock. And that's handy. It's fun too! Add to that an end-of-day cuppa followed by a hot bath, supper in the pub, uninterrupted sleep, a breakfast to build a day's trail-blazing on and the pleasure of being the guests of some of the best hosts one could wish for and you've got luxury. But it costs and, in season, pre-booking is advisable. That means some sort of timetable.

Youth Hostels

Somewhere between the two alternatives are Youth Hostels. You need only carry the same kit as for B&Bs and they're much cheaper. Most provide a full range of services from shop to showers and if you're not

Derwent Water trails offer some fine dirt-tracking for first-time off-roaders in search of the less radical.

the self-catering type, breakfast and evening meal can be a convenient opt-out plus they can even provide a lunch pack. Add to that the best YHA idea – the drying room – and you can see hostels are handy. On the downside, mucking in with a bunch of strangers night-on-night isn't always ideal, accommodation is single sex, in dormitories and sharing a hostel with a bunch of hyper-active juveniles still trying to fight their way free of the education system is not fun! But, all in all, hostels are the best bet and trail-weary bikers are usually well catered for.

The Peak District is well endowed with YHAs and the High Peak Trail has seven along its length. Most are conveniently located so that you can hostel-hop along the entire Trail, though the leap from Elton to Hathersage is quite a haul. Peak District YHAs are listed separately (see p.93). Pre-booking is prudent in high season and be warned; those jolly school parties are a maverick in the accommodation calendar at any time. Many hostels, like B&Bs, have a closed season, so the accommodation logistics of a winter circuit need more careful planning.

ON THE RIDE

Getting There

The great thing about the High Peak Trail is that it begins and ends in Edale. Set right in the heart of the National Park, this picturesque valley has a regular rail service which means you don't have to bring the car. British Rail is not known for being biker-friendly but the Peak National Park people, amongst others, have persuaded BR to provide non-restrictive, free bike transport from Manchester and Sheffield on Sundays. Just turn up and get on! On other days bike carrying capacity is restricted and there's the usual charge, so the key rule is to check, re-check. Booking a bike to Edale is not possible. Edale has a 2-hourly service; 50mns from Manchester Piccadilly and 30mns from Sheffield. For up-to-date travel information ring 0161 832 8353. The A625 runs right past the Vale of Edale, just a stone's throw south in the Hope valley, and provides easy access from the A6 in the west and Sheffield in the east. From the west turn north off the A625 at Windy Knoll (just before the Mam Tor car-park), and from the east turn right, into the mouth of the Vale, at Hope.

Fell-riding

Ride safe. Ride light. Being the new boys on the block mountain bikers have run the gauntlet of being alienated by other countryside users since the word go. The sport has mushroomed and our wilderness areas have witnessed a wheeled invasion – ramblers see us as rivals, environmentalists call us erosionists and farmers fear speeding bikes will frighten stock and uncaring cyclists will flatten crops.

The fact that it's a re-run of early rambler versus landowner conflicts makes no difference. Neither does the fact that the hoary chestnuts of 'tyres tear up trails' and 'bikers are the beasts of the bridleways' are perceived, not proven, concerns of some of our countryside companions. But we're here to stay; entrenched attitudes are already changing and this will come about more quickly if we ride responsibly.

Rights of Way

Although we've taken every care to try and ensure that the mapped High Peak Trail route and the subsidiary Dark Peak and White Peak

Loops will keep your cycling within the law, at the very least the status of some sections is likely to change. Plus, of course, you may get lost so it is as well to be sure of your rights of way.

Off-road cycling is permitted on bridleways, roads used as public paths (RUPPs), by-ways open to all traffic (BOATs), unclassified county roads (Greenways) and designated cycle paths. Some of the North West Water Authority sections of the route are open to us with the landowner's consent and this permissive access may be revoked at any time. Cycling is not permitted on footpaths, open land or on pavements. Do not rely on signposts as reliable indicators of a route's status – local authorities do not always make correct use of bridleway (Blue) and footpath (Yellow) waymarkers. If in doubt dismount. And remember, all land is owned by someone – even the remote moorland areas on this route – and you must take care not to trespass. If a landowner asks you to leave it is in your best interests, no matter what the right and wrong of it may be, to acquiesce.

Of course you may be bowling along a bridleway when up pops a barbed wire fence and the way is barred. It's a tricky situation because your rights are wrapped in a woolly bit of rhetoric which says you can remove the obstacle sufficiently to get past if it is reasonably possible or make a short detour to get round it. The landowner can demand recompense if you cause any damage so clambering over it – often the instinctive reaction – is not a clever thing to do. This doesn't happen often but Rights of Way across farmland do get blocked, ploughed up, are over-planted or are stocked with dangerous animals. Farmers are supposed to provide signed, alternative routes but if you're in doubt don't traipse across regardless. Check with the owner and if you're still forced off the Right of Way report it to the local authority – addresses are given on page 94 – who will take up the matter on your behalf.

Codes of Conduct

In following the High Peak Trail off-road route you will be treading in the tyre tracks of others. If they've careered along, forged furrows across fields, stampeded livestock, left gates gaping and created a trail of havoc and mayhem then you're not going to get a warm reception from the countryside community. Nor is anybody else who follows along unless you follow the Country and Off-road Codes.

Ride Safety

Three's company, not two, and four's fine outdoors in the wilds. In the event of one getting badly injured someone can go for help and someone can stay with the casualty. But ideally two should go for help, not one, which is why four is better. More, and mountain bikers in a bunch can be an intimidating party on a narrow path. Abilities, strength and stamina in any group will vary. Keep within the capacity of everyone, watch your pace and make sure everyone keeps within sight and sound of each other. But don't bunch up, especially on downhills, or there'll be some rear-end wipe-outs. And they can be real nasty! It's always a good idea to wait for stragglers at the top of climbs, at the bottom of tricky descents and at gates. It's in the nature of a strung out group to separate even further at such points so make sure that the young, eager pup out in front is aware of it.

The long shadows of evening in the woods of Crookland.

An idyllic setting for the climb out of the Roych Clough but the trail sweeping through the golden grass is a toughie.

One of the first signs of fatigue is when your normally ebullient companion rides quiet and persistently lags behind. Don't push it. Rest, drink, eat and keep warm – exposure may be just around the corner. Prevention is better than cure. Eat heartily at supper and breakfast, eat lots of carbohydrates, make full use of the various sports recovery drinks and carbo-loading preparations now available – after all you're just as deserving of their benefits as the athletes who advertise the stuff – and make sure you 're-fuel' within an hour or so of arriving at your overnight stop. Try not to ride for more than an hour without having some food – not as easy as it sounds – and drink regularly and drink plenty, before you get thirsty. Don't be overconfident when assessing how much of the High Peak Trail should pass under your tyres during the day. Even the terminally fit will find that forty miles is about as far as they want to go in one day. Always wear enough to keep warm and, if you stop in cold weather, put an extra layer on.

Weather

Out in the wilds, weather will make or break a day. Up on the Pennine ridge it's notoriously variable and in the Peaks it's all in a day's weather to experience sun, sleet, rain, wind, warmth, cold and calm. Maybe the Pennine moors are minor mounds on the world map but it can be as bleak as arctic tundra up on Kinder when winter gets a grip. Bleaklow is as it sounds! It's easy to be lulled into a false sense of security, set out ill-informed and unprepared and end up the subject of a fell rescue operation. Get the most recent weather forecast – telephone numbers are given on page 93 – and make a habit of catching the latest TV weather forecasts. They give a useful overview of what's coming.

Three factors that strangers to the high moors often fail to take into account are altitude, wind and winter. As you climb, temperature falls. Roughly speaking, temperature falls one centigrade degree for every 100m gain in height (3°C per 1000ft) on a clear day, half that fall on a cloudy one. Wind-chill increases with wind strength. In a gentle to moderate breeze (Force 3, about 10mph) wind-chill is about –5°C, about –10°C in a fresh, gusty breeze (Force 5, about 20mph) and –15°C in a really strong wind (Force 7, about 30mph). For example on a clear, calm day the temperature up by Edale Cross will be about 3°C colder than down in the garden of Edale YHA. Add in the cooling effect of the inevitable wind that whips across this col, say a brisk breeze, and up by the Cross temperatures will dip a chilling 12°C or so! No wonder most people seek shelter behind the stone walls! Even in summer the temperature frequently falls to 7°C, in mid-winter we're talking down another 10–14°C. That's way below zero! Makes you think, doesn't it?

It would be foolish to venture out into the Dark Peak if gale force winds are forecast knowing that they'll be more ferocious on the higher fells. Take a furlough and live to bike another day. And be prepared to take an unplanned detour if the weather deteriorates badly whilst you're out. Forecasts give temperatures but it's as well to bear in mind, when planning a departure date, that winter temperatures will be 10–15°C colder than summer ones. Nippy!

Losing your Way

Navigation can be tricky. Keeping on course depends on you, and preferably your companions as well, knowing your position at ALL times. Danger zones are forests, open moor and in poor visibility, so take care to read the terrain correctly in these situations and make no assumptions about this or that trail being a 'main' route. One way of coping with poor visibility is to follow a compass bearing to the most distant visible marker – not a sheep because it might walk off! – cycle to it, take another bearing on the next marker, cycle and so on. With very few exceptions you'll be riding on obvious tracks so you are more likely to feel lost than really be lost.

But, despite our best endeavours to keep you on track, there's always a chance you might wander from the route. Nobody intends to get lost and it comes as a shock. Don't panic. Stop. Make sure everybody's with you and then try to work out where you went wrong. Not too far back you'll have been sure of your position. Find it on the map. Naturally you'll have been using your cycle computer to keep a log of point-to-point distances and it's a simple matter of reading the distance off, calculating direction and that'll give you an approximate position. Forgotten to zero the trip distance at the last known point? Then estimate how long ago you were there and in which direction you have travelled during the elapsed time. Allowing for ground conditions, calculate how far you've cycled. Now check your surroundings and see if local landmarks coincide with your findings. If you're still unsure and visibility is poor then stay put until conditions improve.

In an ideal world three distinct landmarks should be recognised for you to be absolutely certain of your locality though, given two, you can still take compass bearings to position yourself. It goes without saying that correct use of the compass and trusting it, not your instincts, is vital.

Accident Procedure

It's vital too that at least one of the party is a qualified first-aider. Ideally all of you should know the fundamentals of first aid. The British Red Cross, St John's Ambulance and St Andrew's Ambulance Societies all run courses so, if you haven't done so already, book into one. One day, somebody will thank you for it.

It can't be over-emphasised that carrying a proper first aid kit with instructions and being a competent first-aider is an essential part of accident procedure. But first aid instructions don't always cover the common illness and injuries associated with wild country mountain biking. These are given overleaf:

Hypothermia

(exposure – the most common cause for rescue calls)

SYMPTOMS:

Complaints of fatigue; cold, visual abnormalities; lethargy, lack of interest; cold, clammy skin, pale in colour; slurred speech; cramps; clumsiness; odd behaviour; out-of-character actions; collapse and coma. Assume exposure if two or more of these symptoms are apparent and treat immediately.

ACTION:

Stop. Do not continue in the hope that you'll find shelter. **Shelter the patient.** Wrap them in extra clothing and put them in the survival bag, with someone else if possible. If you have a sleeping bag then use it as an inner layer. **Warm the patient** with bodily companionship and a warm drink if possible. Easily digested energy food can be given provided the patient is not too drowsy. **Cheer the patient up** – low morale is a contributory factor. Be positive – the rest of the group will be feeling pretty worried. **Rest the patient** for a prolonged period. If there's any doubt about the patient's ability to recover then send for help. **Look for signs of exposure** in other members of the party and signs of frostbite if conditions are severe. **Do not rub** the patient to restore circulation. **Do not give alcohol** – it may cause collapse. In extreme cases, patients sometimes stop breathing so be prepared to give mouth-to-mouth, and if the patient does lose consciousness place them in the recovery position.
Seek Medical Help

Frostbite

(long descents and winds in winter are common causes)

SYMPTOMS:

Prickling pain; numbness; skin may discolour blue or white; skin may feel hard.

ACTION:

Warm the affected area with additional body heat only. Extremities are the most commonly affected areas and can be placed in the armpit or crotch. The face can be covered with dry, gloved hands. **Remove rings**, watches, boots, etc., to ensure free blood flow. **Return to civilisation** and get the patient to hospital if at all possible or get help. **Do not rub** the affected area. **Do not apply heat** from an artificial source. **Do not use a revitalised limb** or the affected tissue will tear.
Seek Medical Help

Heat Exhaustion

(common during periods of sustained effort)

SYMPTOMS:

Pale, sweaty skin; complaints of dizziness, fatigue and headache; cramps; rapid but weak pulse; shallow breathing; fainting.

ACTION:

Shade the patient. Find a cool, shady spot and lie them down. **Cold drinks of water**, slightly salted and with a little sugar if possible, will soon aid recovery. **Seek Medical Help**

Heatstroke

(severe heat exhaustion)

SYMPTOMS:

Restlessness; frequent passing of urine; complaints of dizziness and headache; hot, flushed, dry skin; rapid, strong pulse; fainting.

ACTION:

Cool the patient by placing them in shade and remove their clothing. **Sponge their body** with water until their body temperature drops and they appear to recover.

Seek Medical Help Immediately

Shock

(present in almost all cases of traumatic accidents)

SYMPTOMS:

Pale and pallid skin, especially the lips; rapid, weak pulse; rapid, shallow breathing; cold, sweaty skin; complaints of dizziness and blurred vision; restlessness; yawning, pronounced sighing; fainting.

ACTION:

Reassure the patient. External bleeding or other injuries should be treated simultaneously. **Lie the patient down**, but keep warm and avoid unnecessary movement. **Turn their head to one side. Raise their feet** on a pile of clothes or small rucksack. **Loosen restrictive clothing. Control body temperature** with loose clothing. **Do not give food or drink. Do not apply heat** from an artificial source.

Seek Medical Help Immediately

Dislocation

(elbow, shoulder and knee joints are most at risk)

SYMPTOMS:

Deformity of the joint, especially when compared to the joint on the opposite side of the body; swelling around the joint; lack of mobility; severe pain associated with the joint.

ACTION:

Support the injured limb in a comfortable position.

Use the triangular bandage for arm/shoulder dislocations when the patient can sit or stand, rolled-up clothes for the leg. **Do not try** to manipulate the joint. **Do not move** the affected joint unnecessarily.

Seek Medical Help

Broken Collar Bone

(perhaps the most common MTB fracture)

SYMPTOMS:

Patient supports injured arm against the body; head inclined towards the injured shoulder; lack of mobility in the injured side; swelling at the front of injured shoulder.

ACTION:

Position arm of injured side with fingers up towards the opposite shoulder, palm flat against the body, so far as the patient will allow. Place soft padding between the upper arm and body. Support the arm using the triangular bandage for an elevation sling off the good shoulder that encloses the elbow, forearm and hand. **Secure the arm** against the body with a belt or strap that encircles the body. **Do not move the injured arm** if it is too painful, support against the body in situ.

Seek Medical Help

OUT OF EDALE

We – that's John, Chris and myself – rolled down the drive of Edale YHA in high spirits, hopping speed humps and heading for the fells of the High Peak intent on hammering trails for six solid days. A heady mix of everything from amble-time road and railpath to white-knuckle, slick-rock single-tracking. Brilliant! The trip had been in the planning pot for weeks, now we were here, right in the heart of hills and I just couldn't help but wonder what tales the Trail would spawn before we rode this road again.

Late afternoon sun saw us side-by-side, sauntering along Edale's leafy lane. A light breeze sent the first leaves of fall scuttling across the tarmac and autumnal air, heavy with the scent of reflection, still held sufficient of summer's heat for us to stash the windproofs. Over our right shoulders Kinder's towering edges cut the northern horizon with a rolling rampart of clough and spur. From somewhere amidst those craggy clefts, in another six days, we'd be taking the final plummet of the High Peak Trail loop. It all looked a bit awesome from down here! Our way out of Edale was hidden from view but it was bound to be a big haul as the valley's hemmed in by 1000ft hill climbs in almost every direction! The intellect might have taken this on board but the imagination hadn't.

We quit the lane and took up on the ragged remains of Chapel Gate road. Well it all started innocently enough; the gradient under control and there're even remnants of tarmac here and there. We go through a gate, look up and there's our track, stepping to the skyline in a breathtaking bid to reach over the reptilian ridge of Rushup Edge. I just know that Chris and John, both race-fit and impervious to pain, are going to pedal to the top. Nobody gets off on tarmac, no matter how tatty it is! So, just as I'm sure those two weren't going to weaken and walk, I knew I'd be a trembling, whimpering wreck by the time I'd got to the top. If I got to the top! I did. Just. As the last shred of tarmac gave up the ghost and turned to rubble, a trio of hikers appeared on the horizon and gave me a heaven-sent excuse to take a pit stop. I saw their feet but was too exhausted to lift my head off the handlebar and give them the usual hearty 'Hail fellow travellers, well met!' A dispossessed voice informed me that my companions were just ten minutes ahead, were chatting merrily and would I like some oxygen? Very funny. Not.

A quick glance back, between my legs, showed an upside-down Edale far below. The distant prospect, blurred by haze and hyper-ventilation, hammered home the incredible height gain that I'd achieved and, with quivering quadriceps still aching from the effort, I made the final few yards happy that I'd not wimped out and walked. My legs wished I had though!

I approached Chris and John hoping they'd read my erratic progress across the heath as a careful choice of line and not the mindless wandering of a wasted cyclist. I guess the stark staring eyes and heaving chest gave it away though! We barely got acquainted with Rushup Edge – aptly titled as terrific winds tear over the top – before dropping down to a rocky gully where a notice entreated us to stick to the sunken track. No encouragement needed! Bare rock strata and rubble arranged in a rude flight of steps gave us a foretaste of things to come. Technical but not extreme – a case of letting the bike roll and riding with it. An awesome descent and well worth a re-run. But then we hadn't yet seen the route where it dips into Roych Clough. That's edge of the envelope stuff and awesome is the name of the game!

Before then the Roych track trod the contours, clipping spurs and dipping through rivulets in the cloughs. Autumn mists veiled fantastic views, painting the landscape in vague silhouettes that disappeared into the distance. It was a terrific feeling to be out here, dirt-tracking across the fells with day-on-day of excellent off-roading in prospect. Unique to long-distance riding.

Easy riding invited cheerful banter but a couple of steep steps cut the chat and it was eyes down, bike skipping for a serious, slippery descent down to the Roych beck. We all dabbed. Chris got dumped – poleaxed and still clipped in the pedals, he lay immobilised like a felled tree until we freed his feet. John, sporting an ear-to-ear grin, was in his element but even he walked the last few yards of rubble-strewn single-track to the stream.

The climb out was no less demanding. Random rubble and rutted cart track not only tested traction but the ping-pong effect had us zig-zagging crazily in an effort to stay on course. Chris, with a wealth of power built on a racing pedigree, kept in line and climbed to crest the col at South Head. While he languished in the last rays from a setting sun, admiring the spectacular scenery, John and I struggled, staggering from bank to bank, legs aching and cursing Chris for being so insensitive as to have stayed in the saddle. That meant we had to too! But life's too short to be so serious and when John suddenly careered off the track – again – all my motive effort evaporated in laughter!

Gravity was in league with us again and, in a burst of unseemly exuberance, I hammered down the empty track below Mount Famine (names hereabouts have a hardness born of a harsh history), skipping every dip big enough to cast a shadow, hopping rocks and revelling in the outright freedom of this off-road thing. That's until a telltale 'chafe-chafe' emanating from the rear wheel put an end to party time. A dented rim. A quick bit of trail-side cold forging with a lump of millstone grit and the wheel was fit for a limp home. On past Peep-O-Day for some serious height gain with a final foray up steep, stepped grass single-track that was sheer torture for tired limbs. Down to Gowhole in the gathering gloom where Chris missed the turning by Brownhill Farm and won an extra climb as a reward for his carry on. Then we had a manic meeting with some suicidal chickens. They ran amok, squawking madly, heads down and playing Russian roulette with the spinning rubber that bore down on them. Feathers fluttered in the half-light but happily we left the chickens flustered not flattened!

Light was fading fast by the time we passed Taxal and climbing single-track with no clear idea of what was making your bike turn bronco was an interesting experience if exasperating. Our sudden appearance in the pools of light that flooded the yard of Oldfield Farm sent the chained dogs insane. Blazing eyes, snarling teeth and a barrage of barking surrounded us. Thankfully, into the dark embrace of Hoo Moor plantation we left the mad, sad dogs behind – though their barking echoed up the Goyt valley for long after we'd gone – and followed a pale trail between the trees. We had lights but there was no need for them. Our wandering white track stood out in stark contrast to the pitch black pines so it was obvious where it went.

Joining tarmac once more we had some close encounters with the roadside and decided to switch on the lights. Instant illumination and there, caught like a rabbit in the beam, stood a startled lad astride a moped. Instant panic! Terrified, he tried desperately to kick-start the machine. We were miles up the valley by the time he succeeded!

Road riding with three watts of light between us was amusing but nothing compared to taking on the off-road descent into Buxton. Trying to read the trail ahead was a real nightmare. Alarming shadows delineated drop-offs that didn't exist; then they did! Taking it slow

Early in the first day on the radical descent into the Roych Clough where boulder-strewn steps add a technical edge.

almost made it worse. With no momentum to carry us through, modest ruts turned into radical wheel grabbers and, with no references to gauge the gradient every dip caught us by surprise. I still wonder how we made it with no wipe-outs, but we did. We spun down the slick, smooth tarmac beneath the streetlamps of Buxton in time for a very late supper at the hostel. I didn't tell the other two that what we'd just come down was our way back out of Buxton on the morrow!

Goyt to Gradbach

From town the track up out of Buxton looked like a real calf-grinder. In the event, we re-acquainted ourselves with the Goyt valley without too much effort – strong tailwinds gave us a bit of a turbo-boost – and in the cold light of day our antics during the previous night's descent seemed distinctly over-played. Never mind, it was an evening of exploits we'll long remember. A lone car that, in the dark, we thought housed a courting couple turned out to be an empty, rusted wreck. Surrounded by bleak moorland, abandoned beside a lonely track with not a soul in sight it lent the landscape an Armageddon air. For a second we felt like sole survivors.

With that friendly following wind we cruised up to the 'Cat and Fiddle' (known to us as the 'Mog and Meddle'). A pub fortuitously placed in the middle of a forsaken, featureless tract of the fells beside a busy highway. No doubt many a fellow traveller has sought refuge from winter's heat-seeking winds but it was a bit early in the day for a bevy so we passed by. And on for a high-speed swoop on some superswift tarmac to Bottom-of-the-Oven. Chris got cocky, adopted an aerodynamic ski-tuck (one hand behind the back, one on the bar and chin on the stem), hit 40mph in freewheel when a sudden sidewind slewed him across the road for a quick dice with the ditch! But the Gods smiled on him and he escaped with a bit of wheel wobble and a missed heartbeat or two.

We all wimped out on the climb to Macclesfield Forest (the hamlet not the trees); it was short, sharp, near vertical and covered in angular lumps of crushed hard-core. By now the wind had worked itself up into a hoolee, making a horrendous, banshee din as it whistled over our heads. Thankfully our rocky route over the hill was well sheltered from the furore but copious amounts of loose stone turned it into a capricious climb. Chris rose to the challenge, stormed up the hill to leave John and me doing a ping-pong routine in a vain effort to reel him in. Much of the descent to Clough House (clough being Peakish for valley, there's more than one Clough House hereabouts!) turned out to be tarmac – a bit disappointing – but a radical zig-zag in the valley bottom added some unexpected spice. Be warned. Cut the speed or you'll wipe out!

Single-tracking was all the sweeter after the tarmac. We single-filed along the overgrown pathway, grabbed some air in the gullies below Tegg's Nose, crossed the stream and got back to track on the run past the placid waters of Teggsnose Reservoir. A big orienteering event was on and exhausted runners, eyes staring, chests heaving, were falling out of the Forest and stumbling about the road in various states of collapse. One poor girl, just twenty yards from the finish, was so wasted she hadn't a clue where she was. John set her right and she limped off toward the line. Funny folk, orienteers. Lucky I don't have the legs for it!

The road led us round the back end of Ridgegate Reservoir where a new NWWA (North West Water Authority) cycle-route peeled off into the pines for an exacting ascent up forest fire-road. A lone crow circled above the canopy, escorting our little convoy, cawing. Or was it cackling in wry amusement at our endless struggle against gravity and mud suck? After a brief bog-trot – the NWWA's trail was not quite complete – gravity was going our way for once, we spun cranks to enjoy a woodland roller-coaster to the road, followed by a delightful wander down a winding lane alongside Clough Brook. An almost forgotten county unclassified track leads up Cumberland Brook valley. Firm at first, it soon degenerates into a challenging pot-pourri of shattered rock, steps and pot holes to test traction and climbing tenacity to the limit. The only way to handle this adverse aggregate is to get angry then let aggravated power get you through. Picking the right line helps too!

The A54 was oddly quiet for such an expanse of tarmac. It has a habit of slipping off fellsides and consequently enjoys long periods of disuse – when we passed by it was at 'No Through Road' status. A very tricky bit of McAdam gave us a dip 'n dive ride down Holt Farm's drive to pick up the bridleway to Three Shires Head. It kicked off with a sheep dip – at least, that's what it looked like – which was a bit bizarre. We didn't fancy bathing the bikes so we walked round! Down in the valley of the Dane, sensuous single-track with a technical edge angled down to the famous bridge. Definitely prime time jamming! A plethora of pathways, rocks, ramps, ruts and rubble kicked up the fun factor and unusually, for a Sunday, it was pedestrian-free. Oh! And the scenery's stunning. Quite Cumbrianesque and distinctly Dunnerdale in

Overleaf: The verdant, cultivated farm-scape of Calton pastures – a complete contrast to the Dark Peak moors we met later in the day.

appearance. (Dunnerdale features in both 'The Coast-to-Coast Ride' and 'The Lakeland Loop': Wheelwright's MTB Guides.)

A quick linger on the bridge then we spied a host of hikers coming down the valley. We made a sharp exit, climbing away from the river on another stretch of county unclassified track. Years of neglect had reduced it to shattered single-track – superlative off-roading with an element of trials riding thrown in. We loved every last yard of it, even the boggy bits! John, master of the 'quick-dab-and-continue' routine, got bounced sideways, planted his front wheel up on a wall (accidentally, I hasten to add!), and still managed to stay in the saddle! Impressive! Then, to bring us back to earth with a bump, we hit a watery ravine full of boulders, hacked to destruction by horses and totally unrideable. A bit of a downer to round off the day's off-roading. It all ended at Manor Farm where we were stunned by the sight of an incredibly steep ramp of concrete up to the road. We gawped at it. 'They do cream teas here,' I suggested. But the other two were already heads down, granny-cogging to the top. After that the long downhill to Gradbach Mill was a heaven-sent opportunity to give the legs a bit of a lay-off. Oh no – we had to climb this lot again in the morning!

Mill, Hill and Dale

Dismal drizzle of the collar-creeping kind. Visibility down to 50yds. Yuk! But my companions seemed carefree and in fine fettle. That's until we hit the hill up to Flash. Even Chris complained at the calf-torture! It's so sheer that I had my work cut out to keep the front wheel on the ground. The shop at Manifold Head, on the A53, proved to be a real country store. It seemed to sell everything, including wheel-sized cookies that make ideal trail food. Tightly stacked contours – some serpentine scribbling by the map maker – painted a pretty accurate picture of the precipitous drop into and crazy climb out of the Dove valley at Moor Side. As if the slide down to the stream wasn't bad enough the climb-out's chicanes had been paved. Then Mother Nature had had her wicked way with it; douse it with water, add walkers and we were reduced to hikers with bikes. Chris coined a new MTB term: 'technical push'. We added it, along with 'ping-pong', to our Peak District Dictionary of Off-Road Terminology.

Suddenly, we were in limestone land. The dark, gritty rock familiar to our tyres had turned to white, slick stone, slippery from condensed autumn mists. Beyond Booth Farm was another arduous ascent that took us deeper into dense cloud cover. I could barely see my barends! Out of the swirling mists drifted the buzz of a small motor. Perplexed, we peered into the fog and got a glimpse of a shadowy figure, advancing slowly, head down, oscillating from side-to-side in a classic 'strimming the lawn' motion. Only there was no strimmer! And besides, he's in the middle of a huge field. Weird! We watch, bemused. It dawns on us that the sound source is a little apart from the mysterious man. No strimmer then but what's buzzing? Suddenly a model helicopter appears out of the vapour, almost clipping the turf and turning in a tight circle round our phantom figure. Strange time, strange place and even stranger weather to be flying model planes in! But if that was eccentric, then the hang-gliders and para-gliders we saw vanishing into the vapour had to be a couple of sarnies short of a picnic!

Then it was back down to the Dove valley on some quick, slick tarmac amidst fantastic scenery that we glimpsed through the thinning mists. Shame we hadn't a clear view – there were tantalising hints of deep green dales, grey gorges, craggy mounts and towering cliffs all around but no stunning panoramas. Still, I guess we've got a good excuse for a return trip. Must be a great place to fly over!

We got a last view over the tortuous folds of this unique limestone landscape as we passed by High Wheeldon then it was back to track, literally, on the High Peak Trail railpath for a top-cog, mile-munching cruise to Friden. Despite the drizzle there were a fair few bikers about so on one of those bright white and blue Sunday afternoons, it would be really chock-a-block. Take it real easy if it is, there'll be all sorts of all ages from four to four score years and more out for a pootle.

If the High Peak Trail railpath was 'chalk' then we were knee deep in 'cheese' within five minutes of leaving Friden car-park. Mega mud-plug down in Longdale. Bovine beasties had puddled up a glutinous goo that clogged everything. Treads? Never mind them, I couldn't find the tyres! The bridleway detoured to the valley top. At first a Herculean struggle to the top seemed futile but it was worth it in the end just to enjoy the high-speed, mud-flicking drop back down the dale. Lightened by letting fly a ton or two of loam we rejoiced in being able to ride easy again. But not for long. If we were dispirited by Long Dale's mud-plug then Gratton Dale's mile-long morass was truly Pilgrim's Progress come true. A regular Slough of Despond! Chris carried his bike, boots squelching through the sticky mix. John and I refused to give up in the face of this sea of supine slurry. We were 'in the saddle' boys. All or nothing. Time after time we made valiant, noisy sorties across the gloop until ballooning tyres or giggling got the better of our frantic efforts at maintaining traction. Then we'd grind to a halt, lungs heaving, exhausted. Chris, staggering about beneath his bike, could barely contain his amusement. We all wiped out – Chris included! I'm just glad he was the sole spectator of this farce. Finally, we made the last climb to Elton, Chris complaining that YHAs are always situated at the top of a hill. Not true, but we all agreed at the lack of consideration given to worn out cyclists when the YHA bought their buildings.

Over Haddon to Hathersage

Weatherwise we'd been dealt a bad week. Again we set off with dreary drizzle dampening our brows, dull steel skies and all hint of summer banished in an onset of wintry wetness. We soon warmed up on the ascent to Upper Town. Ouch! It was a rude awakening for laggardly limbs crying out for a more leisurely intro to another day's trail-blazing.

On top of the hill we hit track and from here on the day picked up in leaps and bounds. By now we'd come to appreciate Peakland trails for their technical quota and the day's first bit of dirt was no exception. Anxious to get some off-road rhythm going I took off up front, spinning cranks and winding up the speed on this choice bit of cart track beneath the trees. A low-slung branch hooked my helmet, throwing me off course. It was a close call but momentum carried me through, then the trail took a dive. We were back to shattered track with boulders, bends and big water runnels to give the fun factor a boost. MTB heaven! And with it wet a layer of slime seriously challenged efforts at keeping speed in check and tested my abilities to stay with the bike to extremes. Edge of the envelope stuff. Rear wheel in a 'slip 'n grip' routine. Bends where rivulets had carved brilliant berms – hook up the treads and hammer on through. It was a case of hang on until you hit the road for Rowsley. Mind the quarry lorries. They're big, bad and bowl along the narrow lanes at alarming speeds.

If vision-blurring descents are not your cup of tea then you'll love the

Side-by-side, spinning down delightful, shade-dappled track in the White Peak – High Peak Trail-blazing at its best.

radical road drop into Rowsley. With a couple of chicanes slipped in to give a touch of tyre stutter you'll need to stop off at Caudwells Mill for a cuppa to quieten the nerves. If you missed the views over the Wye valley then there's a second chance with the climb up over Haddon Hall estate. We paused for a breather and vista fix above Aaron Hole Plantation (only noted because it shares the same name as my first-born son). Then it was on and up. This time on seriously steep and slippery single-track that clawed its way into a dark, dank forest. Two thirds of the way up my rear wheel slipped and it was walk time. Chris and John, calf muscles sizzling, continued to the top. Suddenly, the sun burst through the clouds and transformed our dingy tree-scape into a *chiaroscuro* of forest green, bronze and burnished gold. Instant mood change and, with the warmth of the sun on our necks, we sped across Calton Pastures on a molehill ridden ribbon of slick dirt, masquerading as single-track. Half-track more like!

Calton proved to be a popular valley. Loads of people out for a promenade. This put the skids under any hopes of spinning out on the descent to Calton Lees and even riding three abreast proved a touch dicey – I was nearly pitched into the stream when we circled a group of hikers! We took tea and ten at one of Chatsworth's car park kiosks before climbing up onto Beeley Moor. Here we took to tarmac ridge roads, speeding along smooth McAdam and rejoicing in a bit of slipstream and tyre hum for a change. A bit of top cog cart track, straight as a die and with a dash of downhill gradient, was slipped in at Rodknoll. Three abreast and breathless from tearing along the track, we got a real slap of modern motormania when we met the A619. A roaring stream of jugger-nauts and rep-mobiles blaring horns; frantic in their efforts to overtake in the face of oncoming traffic. Seemed like mayhem and murder to us. Chris was so stunned by the suicidal scenario that he went west, when John and I went east, and cycled off alone! Overcome by a deep feeling of isolation he turned to see two dots in the distance, beetling along in the opposite direction and had to crank hard to catch us up!

Thankfully, the Trail only follows trunk roads for short distances and we returned to quiet country roads where we could relax, listen to the larks and enjoy the scenics. Chris reckoned the landscape was reminiscent of his native Cotswolds. Our scenic lane saunter was finished when we hooked up on some fern-bedecked bridleway down by Foxlane Plantations. Low autumn sun enriched the sumptuous colours of the season. Beech, birch and bracken painted a rich tapestry of terracotta, bronze and gold and the damp, woodland air was filled with scents of the season. For once our trail wasn't a test of trials skills, the dale was deserted and gradient was going our way. Time to taste the simple pleasures of slipstream roar and pure, off-road hammertime with the sunlight flickering off swirling leaves launched skywards at our passing. Nose-to-tail we sped down the trail until the drop-off to the stream caught us out! Only instant, instinctive, evasive action saved us from a triple-stack! A convenient cascade proved an ideal bike wash – waterfalls are Nature's very own wash-and-go for wheels – but it wasn't long before our refreshed framesets were muddied again.

The climb to Car Top was up crudely cobbled cart track that tackled the contours head-on. An ancient road where dislodged rocks and water-cut ruts combine with the cobbles to create the Peak's very own version of the famous Paris-Roubais race route. The dank, dilapidated track tested patience as well as pedal power. Even Chris, who seems to climb everything with consummate ease, careered off into the ferns. One bounce too many, I guess. We were into headwinds on the road ride round Totley Moor and took turns to take the brunt of the bracing westerly breeze. Long shadows stretched across the black asphalt, the air was chill and suddenly it was another quick, autumn evening slipping by. Time to press on. It wouldn't do to be dropping off Stanage Edge in the dark!

Houndkirk Moor's heather-clad shoulders are cut across with a pale trail that packs in some unparalleled off-roading. The track splits into a plethora of pathways, each one sporting its own selection of steps, drop-offs and delicious dilemmas and all set against the backdrop of the big city. Sheffield. Brooding beneath a dark blanket of cloud the gloomy metropolis was the antithesis of everything we were enjoying up here. Open moor gilded in the light of a setting sun, our dirt track disappearing into the distance and here we were revelling in the release that's won from riding a rough track to the limits. One last blast took us down to Ringinglow hamlet then it was back to riding lanes that contoured above the city sprawl – remote yet somehow menacing. We weren't sorry to turn west and head back into the hills.

Beyond the Redmires Reservoirs we took up on our last bit of off-

Overleaf: The Burbage Moor RUPP near Houndkirk. This track's a delight to ride any time and well-loved by local MTBers.

roading for the day. A crazily paved RUPP over Stanedge that's thought to be Roman in origin and an interesting exercise in two-wheeled see-sawing. However attractive the paving appeared to be, its rock 'n roll routine soon had me back to riding the rutted track alongside. From Stanedge Pole the ancient road runs straight to Stanage Edge – the famous gritstone bluff that broods over Derwent Dale in a formidable frown that crowns the valley's eastern horizon. Dark storm clouds raced in over the western hills, backlit by fast-moving fans of light from a sun soon to disappear in the marauding gloom. When the approaching storm finally snuffed it out, darkness spread across the Peakland landscape like a Biblical plague. The almost tangible sense of tension and menace was perfect for giving the adrenalin factor a kick as we dropped off the Edge for one of the Peak District's legendary descents. Despite fatigue it was instant, off-road ecstasy. Drops, dips, ruts running in every direction, bedrock steps with a sprinkling of stones to add the essential technical edge. We spun out onto the lanes above Hathersage, arms aching from endless impacts and bright-eyed on adrenalin buzz. We made it to the hostel just as the first spots of rain fell from a sullen sky. A perfect day's off-roading in the Peaks!

Crowden, Here we Come

Yesterday's spell of sunshine was obviously a flash in the pan. A bedpan judging by the wet weather! So we were in for yet another grey day of drizzle, mists and racing rain clouds. Plus, with Langsett YHA closed today, our planned 'easy day in the saddle' had to be shelved; next stop Crowden YHA, nigh on thirty miles off. And my rump was feeling the effects of yesterday's forty miles in the saddle!

Hill tops were hidden in swirling wreaths of sullen vapour but the highly edited views over the Derwent valley were quite exquisite for all that. The trail was quite a ride too; especially the ascent round Ladybower Tor. Squidgey at first, peaty single-track turned into a tough terrace of bedrock and boulders. A bit slick in the wet, testing traction and power control as tyres slipped 'n gripped over glistening gritstone steps. Then it was back to bog and tyre-squelching single-track. We all made the top – me with a dexterous dab or two – to be wowed by the stunning vista over the Upper Derwent valley. The vale spread out from right beneath our feet but, with a wet wind whipping round the corner of Whinstone Lee, this was no place to linger. Buffeted by capricious gusts dished out by the gutsy nor'westerly, traversing the first few yards along the off-camber, boulder-strewn shoulders of Whinstone Tor called for a keen sense of balance. Not easy with back-packs – they have a hankering for gravity suck and a penchant for pitching you over the bars! Two rain-soaked walkers, buried beneath bulging back-packs and dressed in full foul weather kit, watched forlornly as we flashed by. They looked a dismal duo as they plodded on their way, heads bowed and boots squelching on the boggy path. By complete contrast we hummed along the track, delighting in a bit of dexterous bog-hopping, creaming across the fords and playing the trail flow for all it was worth. Walkers in adverse weather seem a woebegotten breed!

We dropped off the contour-hugging track on a bridleway that suddenly split into an array of pathways. Each one born of another walker's wish to keep their boots dry when traversing the bog. They converged on the far side of the clough to create a fun piece of single-track with humps, bends and berms that had us all take time out from gravity. Abruptly it all turned to rubble. John hung a right to skip the scree, rounded a corner and had a close call with a face-plant on a four foot drop-off! His yell warned us off his detour; the original route through the rubbly ravine suddenly seemed a better bet than extra air – big time! Beyond two tumbledown barns the bridleway took a steep, off-camber dive for the Derwent. The day-long drencher had turned paths into slick, brown slivers of sludge across the hillside. A dab on the back brake and the back wheel was slithering sideways sending the bike uphill! It was like riding an Escher landscape! The harder you tried to ride down, the higher you climbed! Chris climbed straight up into a hawthorn bush! Lesson learned. Beware the back brake, it's like switching on the anti-grav drive.

Down in the Derwent valley we cruised along fire-roads that skirt the manmade lakes. But for a sodden group of biker school kids folk were few and far between. And that's unusual here because normally it's a honeypot and, compared to the isolation of the fells, hitting the lake-side trail feels like all hell's been let loose. The reservoir ride was a welcome respite from the radical roller-coaster routine. We could relax, cruise a bit, cream through the puddles, play a bit of 'splash 'n dash' (self-explanatory, soak your partners routine – being able to jump helps), and railroad each other into the boggy bits.

The track quit the cosy confines of the forest, striking out across the open moors on the appropriately named Cold Side. Too warm and wet to be midwinter it was still pretty bleak. Surprising to think that mega-metropoli like Manchester and Sheffield were a mere dozen miles away. Then again a wet Wednesday wouldn't see a lot of tourists along this track. There were sheep though. As we advanced up the spur above Cranberry Clough – the Trail's only carry – a group of curious ovine spectators gazed down on us. Impassively they surveyed our efforts at manhandling the bikes up the near sheer, slippery slope. It was exasperating. Only at the last moment did they each give up their vantage point on the path. That's until we met a ram. Funny how intimidating a wet ram can look when you're looking right up its nose. Not to mention that you're trying to stop sliding back down a 1:1 slope! John, a farmer's son, saved the day by performing a solo version of 'One Man and His Dog' and put the ram to flight. We carried on. At first in a foot deep furrow where a combination of poise and power control were essential to escape a sharp exit or endo. Then our route quit the clough and we had a laborious push along peat-slurry paths to Cut Gate cairn. An interminable slog up bog-ridden bridleway (it dries out pretty quickly so you may well miss out on the pleasures of this particular mud-plug), but it was well worth it for the delights that awaited us on the downside.

Gravity got a grip, put some spin back in the tyres and enticed us along any one of the plethora of pathways that criss-crossed the landscape for a real, fun-time, semi-technical session of single-tracking. Puddles, peat hag or potholes put an end to any chosen route – that was the rub! It was like Russian roulette. A game of chance. Winner takes the lead. For a time! John piled straight into an innocent patch of peat, stopped dead and pitched straight over the bars. Ouch! Chris was shouting 'Save the bike! Save the bike!' Hang on a minute! What about John? Happily he was shaken, not stunned, but the bike really was sinking out of sight! We plucked it from the peaty soup – a soup that had more suck than quicksand – just in time! My Waterloo came when racing to catch the other two as they scooted down the rocky single-track that's etched out of the ragged Mickleden Edge. A rock, a rut, a wheel jammed and I jumped over the bars! A cut calf and a bruise or two but nothing serious.

By the time we made the bridge over the Little Don River our aching

Our trail dipped, the sun set and we slipped into spiritual mood as we cruised down to Old Dam in the Peak Forest.

limbs were agony. Stiff from the jamboree of jolting and jarring it was a blessing to be able to turn the pedals again. Sad that such a legendary descent had to end though! We'll be back one day! The climb-out from the bridge was one-in-nothing-much – even Chris walked it – but that was nothing compared to the long, slow calf-grinder that runs alongside the A628 trans-Pennine trunk road. Cart track, its twin ruts rain-soaked and slicker than a wet squid, it was a demoralising, sodden ascent of mind-numbing intensity. But for Chris's dogged determination to kill that hill we'd have wimped out and given our wobbly legs a walk. Lady Cross marked the end of the incessant fight for traction. Bar a bog or two it was downhill cruising to Crowden. Storm clouds massed on the horizon. Longdendale's deep valley darkened in the gathering gloom; streaming headlamps, a sinuous string of fairylights, highlighted the dark artery of tarmac that's the A628. Time to kick cranks and get off the fells before nightfall.

Last Leg from Longdendale

Low cloud scudding over the fellsides dragged serried ranks of rain across a melancholy landscape. Grim, dim, dismal. That was how our last day on the High Peak Trail greeted Longdendale. Another fine day then! Not to be discouraged by dreary weather we delayed our departure, putting to rights any mechanicals that had been niggling us for the last few days. Still the drizzle persisted so we set off down the Longdendale Trail destined for a soaking. But our buoyant mood must have counted for something. The rain cleared, the cloud lifted and we cruised down the used railway line amusing ourselves by attempting to negotiate the gateless Kissing Gates without dabbing.

Glossop. Just how I'd always imagined it. A town that sounds like its name. Glossop. The borough council had barred bikes and horses from one of its few bridleways and that about sums the place up. Best left behind. We skirt the centre, endure the long haul to Charlesworth, hang a left and are horrified at yet more climbing up Monk's Road. It ran straight into the mist. No end in sight! Stunned silence was the order of the day. Then, by Matley Moor, it was off-road again. Back to the delights of dirt tracking – well deserved after that dispiriting climb. Round by Lantern Pike the path followed a deep furrow, sown with stones and certainly a touch technical with the extra weight on board. My normal recourse is to blast through boulder-strewn stretches but

Chris showed how forethought, focus and a more leisurely pace pay dividends. Didn't stop me dinging a rim on a drainage tunnel though! A bunnyhop that flopped! A hairline crack counselled a cautious approach to rough stuff from now on. Only half a day to go but then we had Jacob's Ladder – a legendary descent of demonic proportions – to get down.

But we hit rubbly, rim-testing track well before that. A walled lane with wall-to-wall rocks. Taking a leaf out of Chris's book I tracked and weaved in fine style, eyes down, dodging stones with a dexterity alien to my normal routine. So preoccupied with picking lines was I that I failed to see an overhanging holly tree waiting to wipe out the unwary biker. Wham! Terminal wobble! Bushwhacked? I was nearly knocked for six but I fought my way clear, the prickly predator clawing madly at my back-pack.

Hayfield has a fine café – The Twenty Trees – so we took ten (more like twenty really!), a hot cuppa or two and treated ourselves to some tasty cakes. Carbo-loading – not! Perusing the map it dawned on us that ahead lay the last climb of our loop. Our High Peak Trail was all but complete. Despite the weather we'd had a brilliant time so it was with a certain regret that we set off up the Kinder valley with just one more climb to conquer. It's a tough ascent. Typical hardcore cart track. Seriously steep in places and scattered with scree. I focused on the rough track ahead, picking lines with care, not daring to glance up at the summit and cursing Chris and John for their dogged determination to ride it all. Up around a bend, not far from Edale Cross, the trail went exponential. Oh no! I sat on the saddle nose, tyre treads tore at the track, spitting grit in heart-stopping salvos that sent the legs into after-burn and the bike into ping-pong mode. Suddenly I slammed into a flat-topped rock, dabbed and stopped dead. Poleaxed at the eleventh hour! Disappointed at the enforced dismount I prepared to push the final few yards on foot, alone. I looked up and there stood my two companions, waiting for their travelworn trailmate to catch up and cycle over the summit in a threesome. We cruised past the Cross, three abreast, to take shelter in the lee of a dry stone wall. The wind was whipping itself up into a frenzy, low cloud capped our horizons and freezing drops of rain splattered against the dark walls of our wind-break. No place to hang about.

We took off for Jacob's Ladder and the final descent. The cloud

The Wye Valley glimpsed between the trees of Manners Wood.

ceiling was dropping fast, swirling mists darkening the landscape and adding an element of drama to the scene. The track over the col was innocuous enough at first then it fell away and the rough track turned into a treacherous, precipitous piece of paved pathway. In the wet it was wickedly slick so we walked. Walked? A technical slip more like! But once past that we weren't going to let gradient and gravity get their way again. Still a mite technical, we took it easy at first, finessing our way through broken bedrock and rubble, until the rocks petered out, ruts appeared and we were in for a fast, slip 'n slide run-out to the river. Totally brilliant! Over the bridge our bridleway was pedestrian-free so we let loose, spun cranks, dipping and weaving along a myriad of lines to enjoy a last, off-road jamming session down to the farm. A brief bit of McAdam rolling rubber-hum and we were back in Edale; we had reached the end of the Trail, still buzzing from the last blast over Jacob's Ladder and with more than just a few tales we were bursting to tell!

The entrance to Cavedale in Castleton hides a spectacular yet intimate limestone gorge.

MAP SECTION

ROUTE ABBREVIATIONS AND INSTRUCTIONS

The route is split into seven days of riding, but this is only a guideline. The highlighted villages and landmarks on the maps correspond to key points in the route directions. A brief description of the day's ride, including parts of the route to watch out for, is provided at the beginning of each day's ride. Overnight stops are suggested but again only as a guideline.
   The instructions are brief and to the point to make them easy to follow while riding. If in any doubt, always refer to the map and check your compass to ensure you are heading in the right direction. Compass directions are given after each turning.
The following abbreviations have been used:

Turn L: Turn left
Turn R: Turn right
SO: Straight on

Note: directions for using the Dark and White Loops are given on Map 13 and instructions on pages 81 & 82.

KEY

 Map Orientation

 Technical Information

 Overnight Stops

 Off-Road Code

NOTE TO THE MAP SECTION:

The maps used are based upon the Ordnance Survey 1:50 000 series which have been reduced by 20%. Therefore, one mile is equivalent to one inch and one kilometre to 1.6 cm.

Kilometres:

| 1 km | 2 km |

Statute miles:

| 1 m | 2 m |

MAP I

DAY I Maps I – 3

EDALE TO BUXTON
29 miles/45km (16m/26km off-road)
3700ft/1120m of climbing
Summits and Passes: Rushup Edge 1610ft/490m;
South Head 1460ft/444m; Chinley Churn 1445ft/440m;
Hoo Moor 1150ft/350m; Goyt's Moss 1570ft/479m.

It's quite a big day so keep an eye on your progress. The spin along Edale is barely enough to loosen the limbs for the leg-busting 800ft climb up Chapel Gate Track. Perhaps a pre-ride stretching session is a wise idea! Or drop your kit off at Buxton on the way to Edale. Either way at first sight it's an awesome prospect. But once you're up there the views are stunning and the off-roading kicks in in the manner it's going to continue for the rest of the trip – a hot pot-pourri of prime time jamming and techno-track with little in the way of spin-time. That's until you reach Goyt Valley when things quieten down. The Roych Clough has a reputation as a serious serpent down which to slip – take care, it bucks a bit, and remember that your balance and braking is adversely affected by the extra weight in the rucksack. If it's May then you'll be treated to a stunning floral display alongside Errwood Reservoir.

LOCATION | ROUTE DIRECTIONS

EDALE

Start at Edale YHA entrance (GR140861) and turn R (SW) for 2.5m/4km, passing through Edale and over River Noe, to pick up gated bridleway track off R (SW). Climb for 1.5m/2.4km up Chapel Gate Track (seriously steep in places), swinging L (S) over spur, to bridleway T-junction then turn R (WSW) for 0.5m/0.8km down sunken track to A625. Fork R (WSW) for 0.12m/0.2km then turn R (WNW), following Roych track for 2m/3.2km

ROYCH CLOUGH

(gets very rubbly and steep into Roych Clough), to bridleway/footpath T-junction. Keep SO (NW) for 0.5m/0.8km to track T-junction and keep SO (NW) again for 1.4m/2.2km, soon to swing L (W then NNW) round South Head (on the last day of the ride you should be traversing the valley 0.75m/1.2km north), with a final run down straight track, to a bridleway X-roads. Turn L (W then SW) for 0.25m/0.4km to the A624, turn L (S) for 110yds/100mts then turn R (W) for 80yds/75mts to keep SO (W) up track 0.6m/1km, keeping L (WSW) at next fork, to Hills Farm. Pass round L (W) side of house then climbing at first (NNW then W) for 0.4m/0.65km to bridleway T-junction at waymarker then swing L (S) for 0.5m/0.8km to bridleway T-junction (marked by a pole), and turn R (WNW) for 0.8m/1.3km to track/C-road X-roads. Go SO (WNW) for 0.4m/0.65km to bridleway/C-road T-junction by Brownhill Farm then turn L (SW then SSW) for 0.7m/1.15km to join C-road on a corner. Turn R (W) for 0.4m/0.65km, under railway, to T-junction then hairpin turn L (SSE then SW) for 0.4m/0.65km up to the A6 (busy road take care!) Go SO (SW) staggered R/L X-roads for 0.4m/0.65km, keeping L (SSW) after 0.25m/0.4km, to then fork L (S) just past Yeardsley Hall for 0.4m/0.65km to Hockerley, keeping L (SSE) after stream. Swing R (S) 0.4m/0.65km, over X-roads in estate, to T-junction. Turn L (E) for 0.3m/0.5km down into Whaley Bridge.

WHALEY BRIDGE Turn R (S) for 0.4m/0.65km to X-roads then turn R (W) on B5470 towards Macclesfield for 0.4m/0.65km then L (S) at T-junction for 1.4m/2.2km passing Taxal church on the way. Turn L (E) for 0.5m/0.8km on gated track, down zig-zag, over stream and up to go through bridle-gate (waymarker) into field on R (SW). Go 0.1m/0.15km across field to gate then swing L (E) up track for 110yds/100mts through gate to fork by barn and keep L (SSE) for 0.3m/0.5km, passing through Oldfield farmyard, to unclassified road. Keep R (S) (effectively SO) through gate then for 1.25m/2km, through forest, to C-road then turn L (ESE) for 3.25m/5.2km, keeping R (S) at T-junction

GOYT VALLEY by Errwood Reservoir, up Goyt valley to Derbyshire Bridge car park and toilets. For Buxton YHA turn L (E) (Note: you will return on this route to rejoin the HPT so memorise it as you go.) on track for 2m/3.2km (watch out for gate 150yds/130mts into descent), to A53 X-roads by Burbage church in Buxton. Swing R (ESE) (effectively SO and it's one-way for the first bit),

MAP I

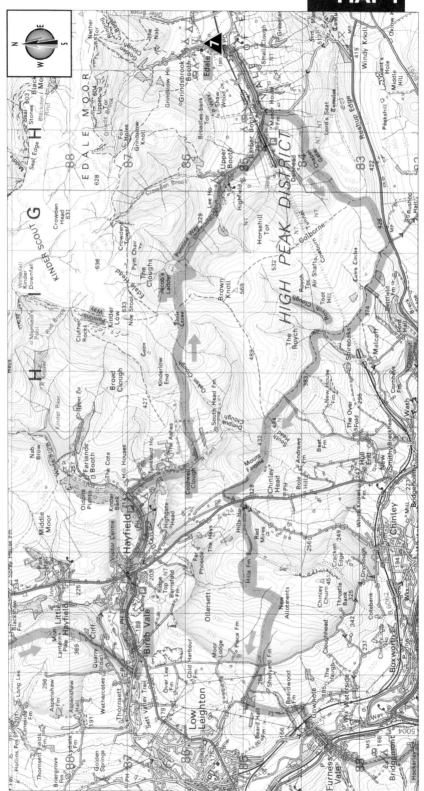

for 1.1m/1.75km to X-roads in town centre then turn R (SE) on the A515 for 0.5m/0.8km to T-junction (it dips sharply here), and there turn R (S) for 50yds/50mts to Buxton YHA. (**Suggested overnight stop**)

DAY 2 Maps 2 – 4

BUXTON TO GRADBACH
22 miles/35km (12m/19km off-road)
3300ft/1010m climbing
Summits and Passes: Goyt's Moss 1570ft/479m;
Cat and Fiddle 1675ft/510m; Macclesfield Forest (E) 1560ft/475m;
Nessit Hill 1310ft/400m; Sparbent 1480ft/450m; Turn Edge
1265ft/385m; Far Brook 1265ft/385m.

Once again there's a fair bit of climbing to do – most of it up tricky bits of track that are technical challenges even when gravity is on your side. If a capricious climb is your meat then dig in and enjoy! The first bit of off-road to come into view is the track storming up over Goyt's Moss – don't despair it's looks worse than it is. The old 'Cat & Fiddle' is a bleak spot – usually windswept too – but the dip to the Bottom-of-the-Oven is an eye-watering, out and out speed-freak's party. Macclesfield Forest is an extremely popular recreational area – please ride with extra care. Given its first public airing through the pages of this book, the **NWWA** permissive cycle-route out of the forest may be subject to changes so please follow the waymarkers. Cumberland Beck – more capricious climbing. Then you're into the Dane valley and some sensuous single-tracking that'll put a smile on your face.

DERBYSHIRE BRIDGE To continue on the HPT from Derbyshire Bridge go (WSW) for 1m/1.6km on C-road to A537 then turn R (NW) for 0.9m/1.4km, passing 'The Cat and Fiddle' pub, to fork L (W) at the next T-junction for 1.2m/1.9km to T-junction in Bottom-of-the-Oven. Turn L (SW) for 0.12m/0.2km then fork R (SW) for 80yds/75mts to T-junction with unclassified road.

MACCLESFIELD FOREST Turn R (NW then W) for 0.3m/0.5km up steep climb to Macclesfield Forest hamlet C-road/unclassified road X-roads then turn R (NW) for 1m/1.6km on track to join tarmac at T-junction. Here turn R (N then NW) for 0.5m/0.8km to A537 and turn L (WSW) for 140yds/125mts to T-junction with unclassified road (the first turn left), at Walker Barn, and turn L (SSW) for 0.9m/1.4km (steep switch-back across valley bottom – take care!), to fork R (SW) onto single-track bridleway just as the lane dips L (E). Follow bridleway for 1m/1.6km, over stream and joining track, to T-junction with C-road in Langley.

LANGLEY Turn L (ESE) for 0.7m/1.15km to T-junction by Ridgegate Reservoir then fork R (ESE) for 0.5m/0.8km, alongside the lake, to next T-junction and turn R (SW) for 0.25m/0.4km to gated track off L (SE). Go through gate (This is the beginning of the NWWA cycle-route through Macclesfield Forest via Ferriser so please follow their waymarkers. These may differ from the route

NESSIT HILL described.), then for 1.25m/2km, over Nessit Hill, to T-junction then fork R (SE then E) for 1.25m/2km roller-coaster ride to gated X-roads with C-road. Turn R (ESE) (towards Wildboarclough), for 0.25m/0.4km to T-junction then turn R (SSE) for 1m/1.6km down valley to Clough House and fork L for 0.1m/0.15km to T-junction with unclassified road. Turn L (E) for 0.7m/1.15km, crossing ford and passing below Cumberland Cottage, up to T-junction then swing R (S) over ford and climb for 0.6m/1km to A54. Turn L (ENE) for 0.3m/0.5km then hairpin turn R (S) on bridleway drive for 0.2m/0.3km to turn R (SW) onto bridleway track through pens at Holt. Continue (S then E then SE) for 0.6m/1km on bridleway over fields then on single-track down the valley to Three Shires Head bridge.

THREE SHIRES HEAD Cross the bridge and swing R (S) onto unclassified road for 0.2m/0.3km climb to fork at gate then keep L (SSW) for 1m/1.6km, swinging L (E then NE) right round Turn Edge hill to join gated tarmac lane, to single-track bridleway off R. Hairpin turn R (S) for 0.5m/0.8km down (steep, narrow and rocky), across footbridge and up past Far Brook Farm (teas available here), to C-road. For Gradbach YHA turn R (W) (Note: you will return on this route to rejoin the HPT so

MAP 2

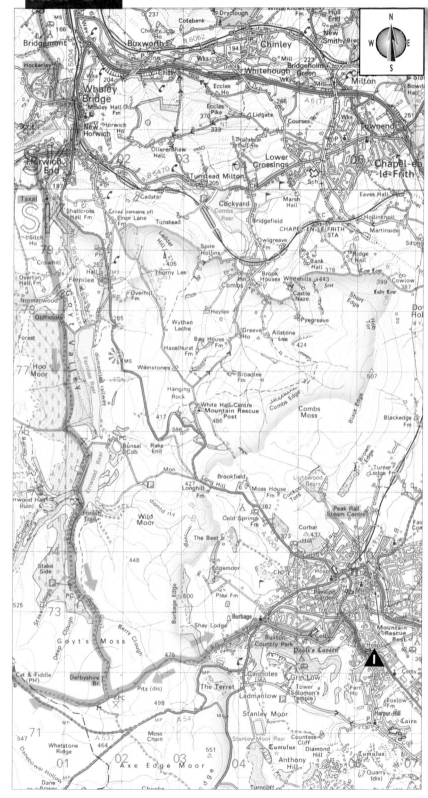

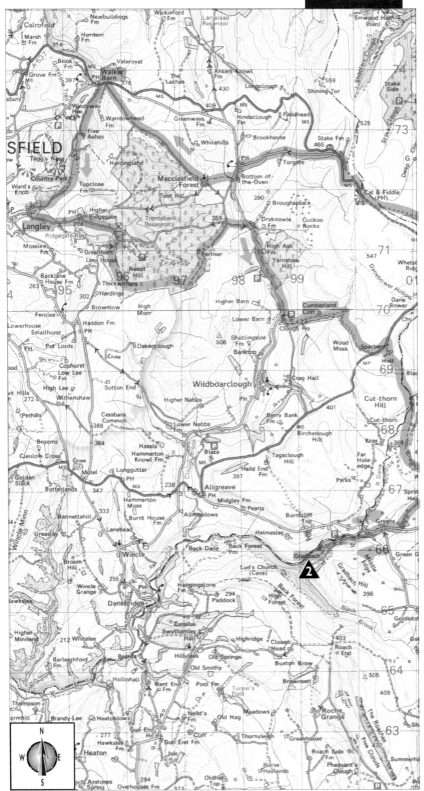

memorise it as you go.) Continue for 1m/1.6km to T-junction then turn R (W) for 0.25m/0.4km going SO (WSW) at next T-junction to fork L (WSW) for 0.6m/1km up dead-end lane to Gradbach YHA. **(Suggested overnight stop)**

OFF-ROAD CODE

● **Enjoy the countryside and respect its life and work**

● **Guard against all risk of fire**

Rock strata and rubble form the rude flight of steps that's Rushup's ridge track.

DAY 3 Maps 3 – 5

GRADBACH TO ELTON
25 miles/40km (15m/24km off-road)
2300ft/700m climbing
Summits and Passes: Flash 1545ft/471m;
High Edge 1445ft/440m; Wheeldon 1320ft/402m;
Long Dale Edge 1000ft/305m.

Flash. Even motorists quake at the word and when the hostel warden heard that we were heading that way he looked at our legs and laughed. It's a bit of a wheel-lifter and packs in half of today's height gain in one crack! So get those limbs stretched before you start. By lunchtime the hard graft is done and you can relax. We're into White Peak land. Limestone. Gritstone gives a leach-like grip even when wet – you can rely on the rubber to hook up when things look hairy. But limestone's more slippery than slug slime if there's the slightest hint of H2O glistening your treads. Watch it! And the mud is goo glue with build qualities better than Blu-Tac! A lesson we learned in Long Dale. Keep an eye on the scenery – it's sublime. Remember also that Elton is a self-catering hostel and buy some food before you get there.

FLASH　To continue on the HPT from Far Brook Farm turn L (NE) for 1m/1.6km, up through Flash to A53 then turn L (NNE) for 0.25m/0.4km to T-junction (good provisions shop here. Closed Mon-Tues), and turn R (SE) for 1m/1.6km, passing two T-junctions off L, to X-roads. Turn L (NE then E) for 0.7m/1.15km, towards Moorside Farm, to turn L (NW) on single-track bridleway for 1.5m/2.4km, over pack-horse bridge to swing L (NW) up switch-back unclassified road and past Leycote and Booth farms, to T-junction with C-road below High Edge.

HIGH EDGE　Turn R (SE) for 2.3m/3.7km to Glutton Bridge staggered X-roads then zig-zag L/R (effectively SO), (ESE) onto gated unclassified road for 1.1m/1.75km, passing through Underhill Farm, to T-junction with C-road and turn L (N) for 0.4m/0.65km to hairpin turn R (E) for 0.2m/0.3km up unclassified road to C-road. Turn R (SE) for 0.3m/0.5km to fork L (ESE then NE) at next T-

MAP 4

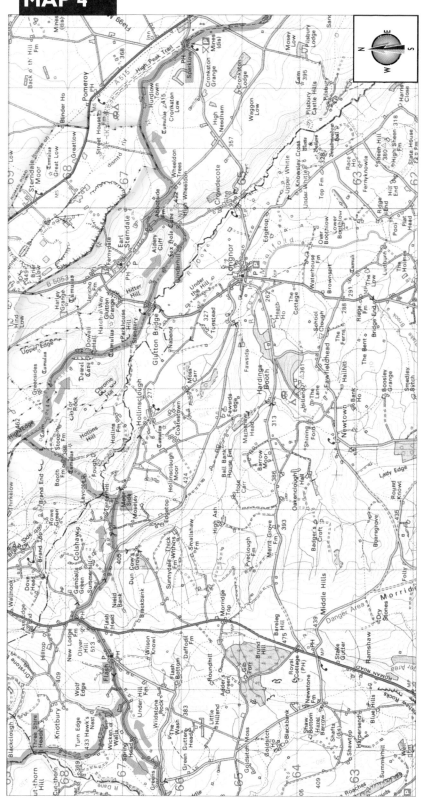

MAP 5

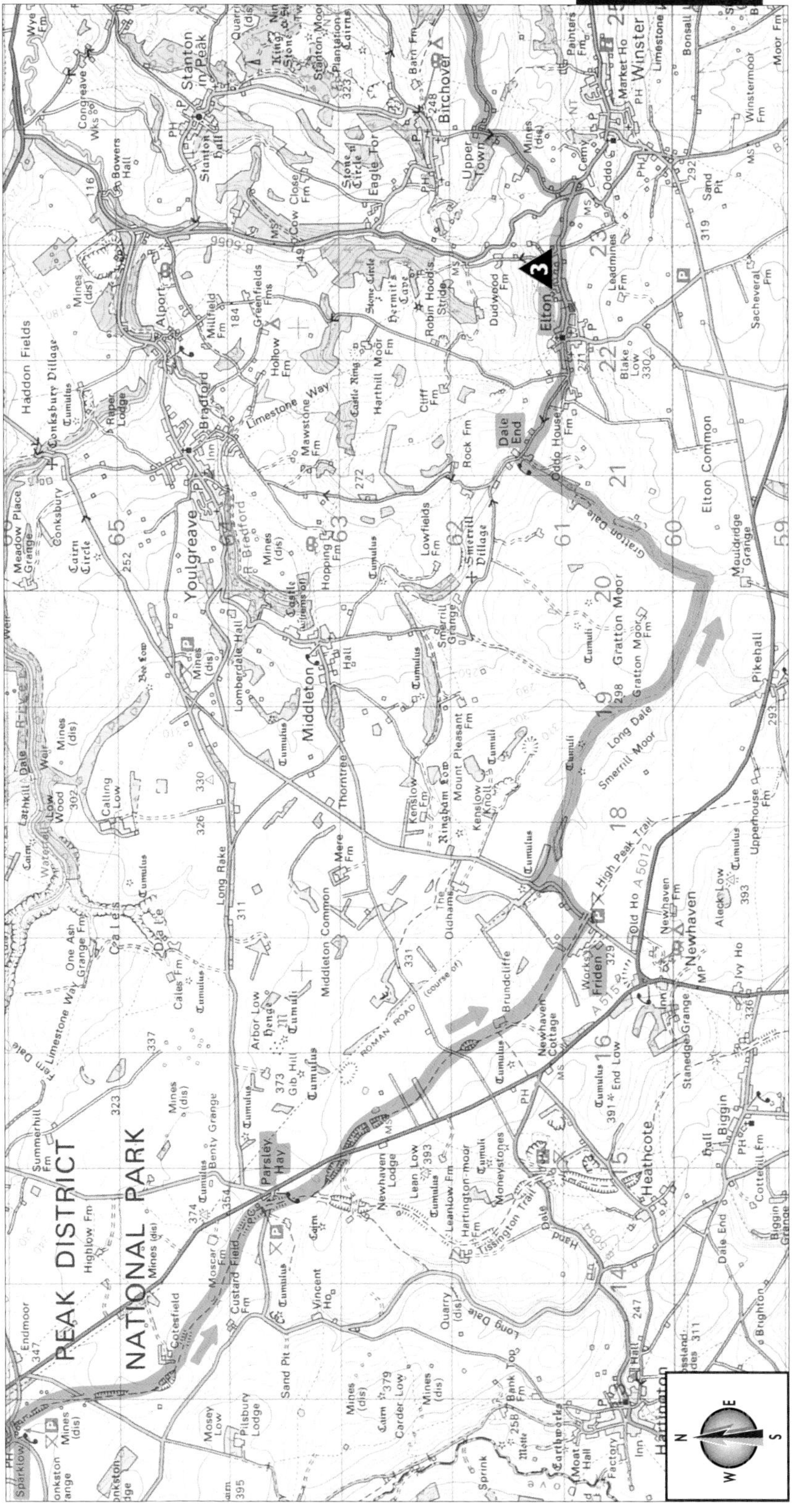

PEAK DISTRICT
NATIONAL PARK
Sparklow
Endmoor
Cotesfield
Custard Field Fm
Moscar Fm
Highlow Fm
Summerhill Fm
Mines (dis)
Benty Grange
Parsley Hay
Newhaven Lodge
Lean Low
Leanlow Fm
Hartington-moor Fm
Moneystones
Tissington Trail
Vincent Ho
Quarry (dis)
Long Dale
Hand Dale
Heathcote
Biggin
Hall
Cottetill Fm
Biggin Grange
Dale End
Brighton
Hartington
Hall
Inn
Factory
Moat Hall
Earthworks
Sprink
Bank Top Fm
Carder Low
Mosey Low
Pilsbury Lodge
Sand Pit
Arbor Low
Henge
Gib Hill
Tumulus
Tumuli
ROMAN ROAD (course of)
Middleton Common
Brundcliffe
Newhaven Cottage
End Low
Staneledge Grange
Ivy Ho
Newhaven
Friden
Works
Old Ho
High Peak Trail
A 5012
A 515
Aleck Low
Upperhouse Fm
The Oldhams
Mere Fm
Long Rake
Cales Fm
Cales Dale
One Ash Grange Fm
Limestone Way
Calling Low
Lathkill Dale
River
Low Wood
Weir
Mines (dis)
Youlgreave
Bradford
Lomberdale Hall
Middleton
Thorntree
Hall
Castle (remains of)
Kenslow Fm
Ringham Low
Mount Pleasant Fm
Kenslow Knoll
Smerrill Moor
Long Dale
Gratton Moor
Gratton Moor Fm
Gratton Dale
Pikehall
Smerrill Grange
Smerrill Village
Lowfields Fm
Hopping Fm
Mawstone Fm
Rock Fm
Dale End
Oddo House Fm
Elton Common
Mouldridge Grange
Cliff Fm
Harthill Moor Fm
Castle Ring
Stone Circle
Hermit's Cave
Robin Hood's Stride
Dudwood Fm
Elton
Blake Low
Leadmines Fm
Sacheveral Fm
Hollow Fm
Greenfields Fms
Millfield Fm
Alport
Haddon Fields
Conksbury Village
Conksbury
Meadow Place Grange
Cairn Circle
Bowers Hall
Congreave Wks
Stanton Hall
Stanton in Peak
Cow Close Fm
Stone Circle
Eagle Tor
Birchover
Upper Town
Winster
Market Ho
Oddo
Cemy
Winstermoor Fm
Moor Fm
Sand Pit
Painters Fm
Stanton Moor
Plantation
Barn Fm
B 5056
B 5054
3

junction for 2m/3.2km, passing footpath access track to the 'High Peak Trail rail-path' off L (N), to T-junction at Sparklow Inn.

'HIGH PEAK TRAIL RAIL-PATH' Turn L (E) to join 'High Peak Trail rail-path' via the car-park (effectively going SO; SSE), (there'll be lots of less experienced cyclists riding so please take extra care), and continue (SSE) for 2.5m/4km, past

PARSLEY HAY Parsley Hay (Cycle Hire Centre can provide basic bike bits in emergencies. There're also toilets and refreshments), to T-junction and fork L (SSE) for 2.5m/4km, under A515, to Friden.

Leave 'High Peak Trail rail-path' via car-park to turn R (NE) on C-road (effectively going L from rail-path) for 0.4m/0.65km to fork R (NNW then ESE) on single-track unclassified road (easy to miss it's off the first L bend. Get to the valley bottom and you've over-shot.), for 0.7m/1.15km, along valley bottom (mud plug), to gateway by end of plantation.

LONG DALE Swing L (ENE) for 110yds/100mts, climbing above Long Dale on feint single-track, to fence then swing R (SE) for 0.5m/0.8km along lip of valley and then swing R (SSE) for 0.15m/0.25km down grassy descent to bridle-gate in valley bottom. Swing L (SSE then SE) for 0.9m/1.4km on obvious single-track bridleway then turn L (NNE) through bridle-gates, for 1.4m/2.2km (rocky mud plug) to T-junction with C-road at Dale End.

Turn R (SE) for 1m/1.6km to Elton YHA.

(Suggested overnight stop – self-catering hostel)

OFF-ROAD CODE
- **Fasten all gates**
- **Keep dogs under control**

DAY 4 Maps 5 – 8

ELTON TO HATHERSAGE
38 miles/61km (20m/32km off-road)
3725ft/1135m climbing
Summits and Passes: Beeley Moor 1181ft/360m;
Houndkirk Moor 1390ft/424m; Stanedge Pole
1430ft/436m.

There's not a lot of accommodation on the western fringes of
Sheffield so that's why we're heading for Hathersage. OK, it's a
long haul but half of it's on McAdam which means that the miles
will slip serenely under the tyres (unless the wind's in the north
eastern quadrant in which case tarmaccing can be a slog). In
between the tarmac there's some supreme off-roading with the
rough route out of Upper Town an excellent opener. The Derwent
valley is awash with strollers in season so ease up a bit – there's
plenty of prime time trail-blazing later in the day on the cart
tracks that cross Houndkirk and Hallam Moors. With luck you'll
finish the day finessing your way down Stanage Edge, a smile on
your face, a lump in your throat and a sensational sunset for an
inspiring backdrop.

ELTON	To continue on the HPT go SO (E) for 0.8m/1.3km, over B5056, to turn L (N) for 0.8m/1.3km to Upper Town then turn R (E then S then E again) for 1.4m/2.2km on unclassified road (tricky descent if wet), to staggered track X-roads where you zig-zag R/L (effectively SO), (E) for 0.5m/0.8km to T-junction with C-road. Turn L (WNW) for 1.6m/2.6km (quarry lorries use these lanes so take care), keeping R through Stanton Lees hamlet, to T-junction then fork R (NNE) for 1m/1.6km to T-junction in Pilhough.
ROWSLEY	Turn R (NE) for 0.8m/1.3km on descent to staggered X-roads on the A6 in Rowsley (Caudwells Mill Centre has a cafe and there's a shop in the village), then zig-zag L/R (effectively SO) (NW) for 0.75m/1.2km, joining bridleway track, to track T-junction then swing L (WNW) to contour for 0.5m/0.8km to a staggered track X-roads. Turn R (N) up single-track bridleway into forest for 0.25m/0.4km to T-junction then swing L (NW) for 110yds/100mts to another T-junction

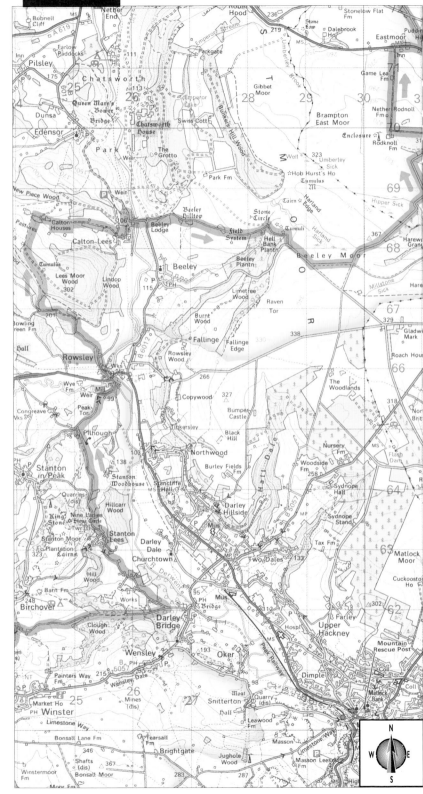

MAP 6

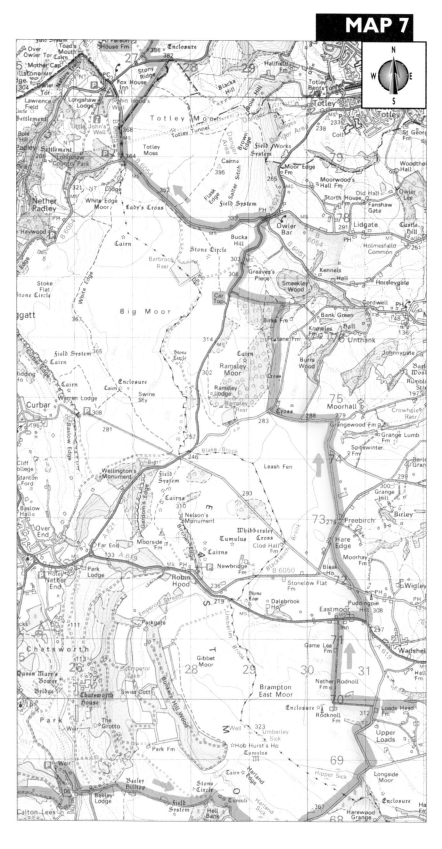

MAP 7

and turn R (NE then NW) for 0.5m/0.8km, onto ridge top track, to edge of forest.

CALTON PASTURES Turn R (NE) for 50yds/50mts to waymarker and through gate onto Calton Pastures. Go SO (NE) for 0.4m/0.65km on single-track bridleway to go through gate between Calton Plantations (gloopy here), then turn R (ESE) for 0.1m/0.15km, alongside plantation, then turn R (SE then ESE) through gate for 0.9m/1.4km past Calton Houses, down track to T-junction with tarmac unclassified road.

BEELEY MOOR Fork L (SE then N) for 0.4m/0.65km, through car-park (there's a seasonal kiosk here), to B6012 then turn R (SSE) for 0.3m/0.5km, over River Derwent, to fork L (NE then E) at Beeley Lodge for 1.8m/2.9km on unclassified road, tarmac at first, to T-junction with C-road on Beeley Moor. Turn L (SE) for 0.3m/0.5km to first T-junction then turn L (E) for 0.4m/0.65km to X-roads and there turn L (NNE) again for 1.2m/1.9km to the next T-junction and turn L (NNW) for 0.8m/1.3km to T-junction with unclassified road at Loads Head Farm.

LOADS HEAD FARM Turn L (W) for 0.5m/0.8km to T-junction then turn R (N) for 1m/1.6km to A619 (very busy road – take extra care when crossing). Turn R (E) for 0.3m/0.5km to staggered X-roads then turn L (N) for 1m/1.6km, SO (NW) at next X-roads, to T-junction with B6050 and turn R (NNE) for 0.2m/0.3km to next T-junction at Freebirch then turn L (N) for 1.1m/1.75km, SO (N) at next T-junction, to another T-junction. Turn L (W) for 0.8m/1.3km, SO (W) at next T-junction, to X-roads with gated bridleway. Fork R (N) onto bridleway for 0.2m/0.3km then keep R (NNE) on bridleway at this fork then on for 0.9m/1.4km down valley to stream. (Beware. Can come up suddenly.)

DERWENT VALLEY Go SO (N) over stream for 0.1m/0.15km to go through gate then turn L (W) for 0.6m/1km up to A621 at Car Top and turn R (NNE) for 0.9m/1.4km to roundabout then turn L (W) (towards Hathersage), for 2m/3.2km to T-junction overlooking Derwent valley. Swing R (N) on B6055 for 0.3m/0.5km then fork R (NE) on B6450 for 0.8m/1.3km to A625 and turn L (W) (towards

MAP 8

Hathersage) for 0.25m/0.4km to T-junction with BOAT. Turn R (NW) for 0.1m/0.15km to X-roads with Parson's House drive then turn R (NE) on obvious track for 1.7m/2.7km to vague X-roads and go SO (NE) for 0.6m/1km to T-junction with C-road.

RINGINGLOW Keep L (NNE) for 0.12m/0.2km to staggered X-roads in Ringinglow then zig-zag L/R (effectively swing L), (NW) on contouring lane for 2m/3.2km, keeping L at junctions, to T-junction at bottom of hill and turn L (W then N) for 0.5m/0.8km to another T-junction.

REDMIRE RESERVOIRS Turn L (W) for 1.4m/2.2km, round Redmire Reservoirs, to swing R (SW then W) for 1.2m/1.9km on BOAT, passing Stanedge Pole, to Stanage Edge. Swing R (NW) for 1.3m/2.1km, soon to drop down tricky descent, on obvious track to C-road. Go SO (S) (towards Hathersage) for 0.2m/0.3km to T-junction. To continue the HPT, missing out Hathersage, you can fork R (WSW then WNW) for 2m/3.2km to join the A6013 N-bound for 1m/1.6km to the A57.

To go down to Hathersage YHA keep L (S) for 1.1m/1.75km to T-junction and swing R (S) for 0.5m/0.8km to T-junction in village then turn L (ESE) for 0.2m/0.3km to A625 for hairpin turn R (W) for 80yds/75mts to YHA. **(Suggested overnight stop)**

Carlton Pastures' bridleways are very popular with ramblers, so ride with care.

MAP 8

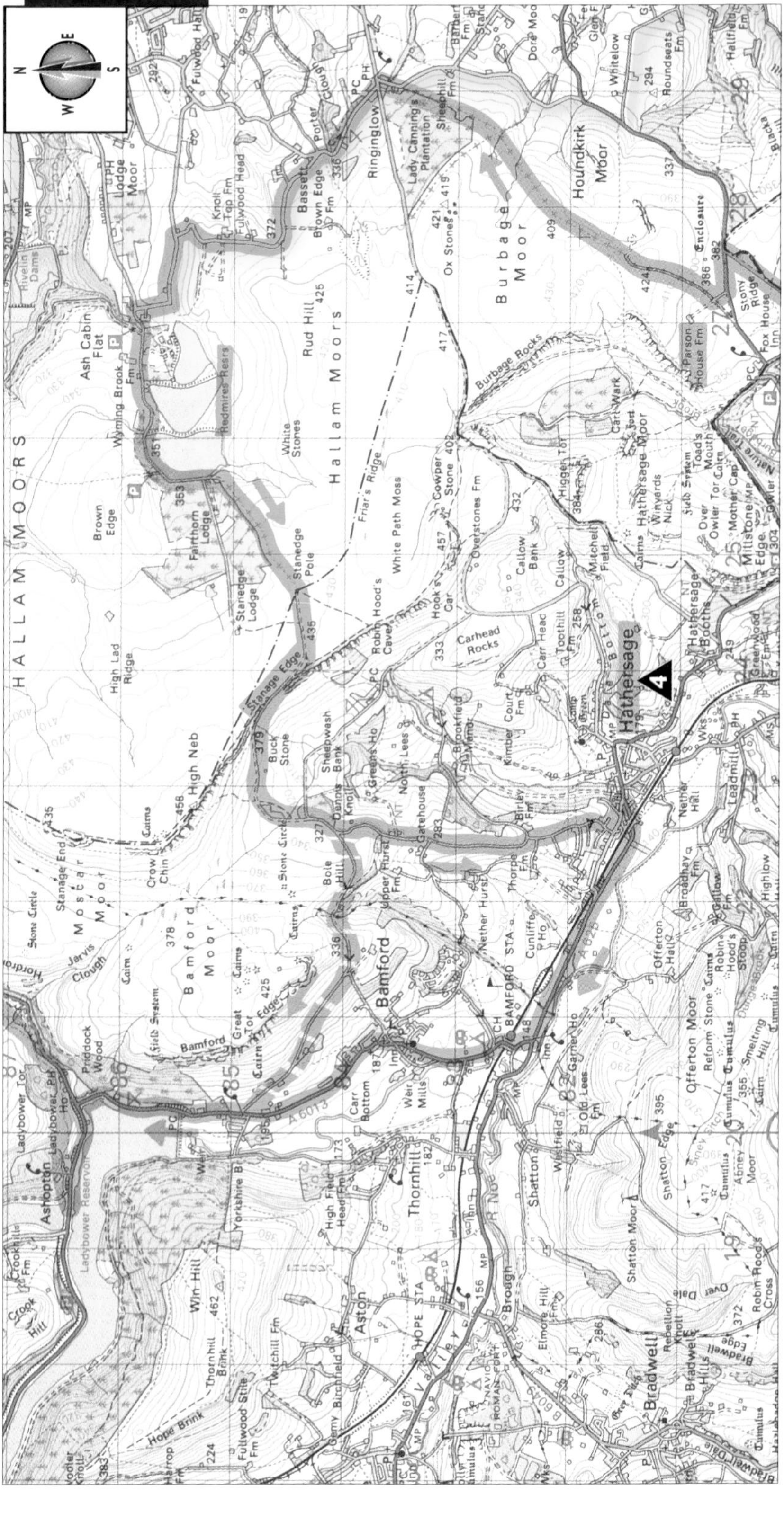
N
E
S
W
HALLAM MOORS
Hallam Moors
Burbage Moor
Houndkirk Moor
Ringinglow
Lady Canning's Plantation
Sheephill Fm
Bassett
Brown Edge Fm
Knoll Top Fm
Fulwood Head
Lodge Moor
Fulwood Hall
Rivelin Dams
Ash Cabin Flat
Wyming Brook Fm
Redmires Resrs
Rud Hill
White Stones
Brown Edge
Fairthorn Lodge
Stanedge Pole
Stanage Lodge
Friar's Ridge
White Path Moss
Cowper Stone
Burbage Rocks
Ox Stones
Overstones Fm
Higger Tor
Carl Wark
Hathersage Moor
Toad's Mouth
Winyards Nick
Over Owler Tor
Mother Cap
Millstone Edge
Parson House Fm
Fox House Inn
Stony Ridge
Enclosure
Roundseats Fm
Whitelow
Hallfield Fm
High Lad Ridge
High Neb
Stanage Edge
Robin Hood's Cave
Hook's Car
Carhead Rocks
Callow Bank
Callow
Mitchell Field
Toothill Fm
Carr Head
Hathersage
Hathersage Booths
Dale Bottom
Greenwood Fm
Buck Stone
Sheepwash Bank
Green's Ho
North Lees
Brookfield Manor
Kimber Court Fm
Birley Fm
Dennis Knoll
Gatehouse
Stanage End
Moscar Moor
Crow Chin
Cairns
Stone Circle
Bole Hill
Upper Hurst Fm
Nether Hurst
Thorpe Fm
Cunliffe Ho
Bamford Moor
Great Tor
Bamford Edge
Jarvis Clough
Bamford
BAMFORD STA
Nether Hall
Broadhay Fm
Leadmill
Offerton Hall
Robin Hood's Stoop
Offerton Moor
Reform Stone
Smelting Hill
Highlow
Priddock Wood
Ladybower Tor
Ladybower Reservoir
Ashopton
Crook Hill
Crookhill Fm
Win Hill
Yorkshire Br
Carr Bottom
Weir Mills
High Field Head Fm
Thornhill
Shatton
Westfield
Old Lees Fm
Garner Ho
Shatton Edge
Shatton Moor
Abney Moor
Aston
HOPE STA
Brough
Elmore Hill Fm
Bradwell
Bradwell Edge
Rebellion Knoll
Over Dale
Robin Hood's Cross
Thornhill Brink
Twitchill Fm
Fulwood Stile Fm
Hope Brink
A 6013
A 625
4

MAP 9

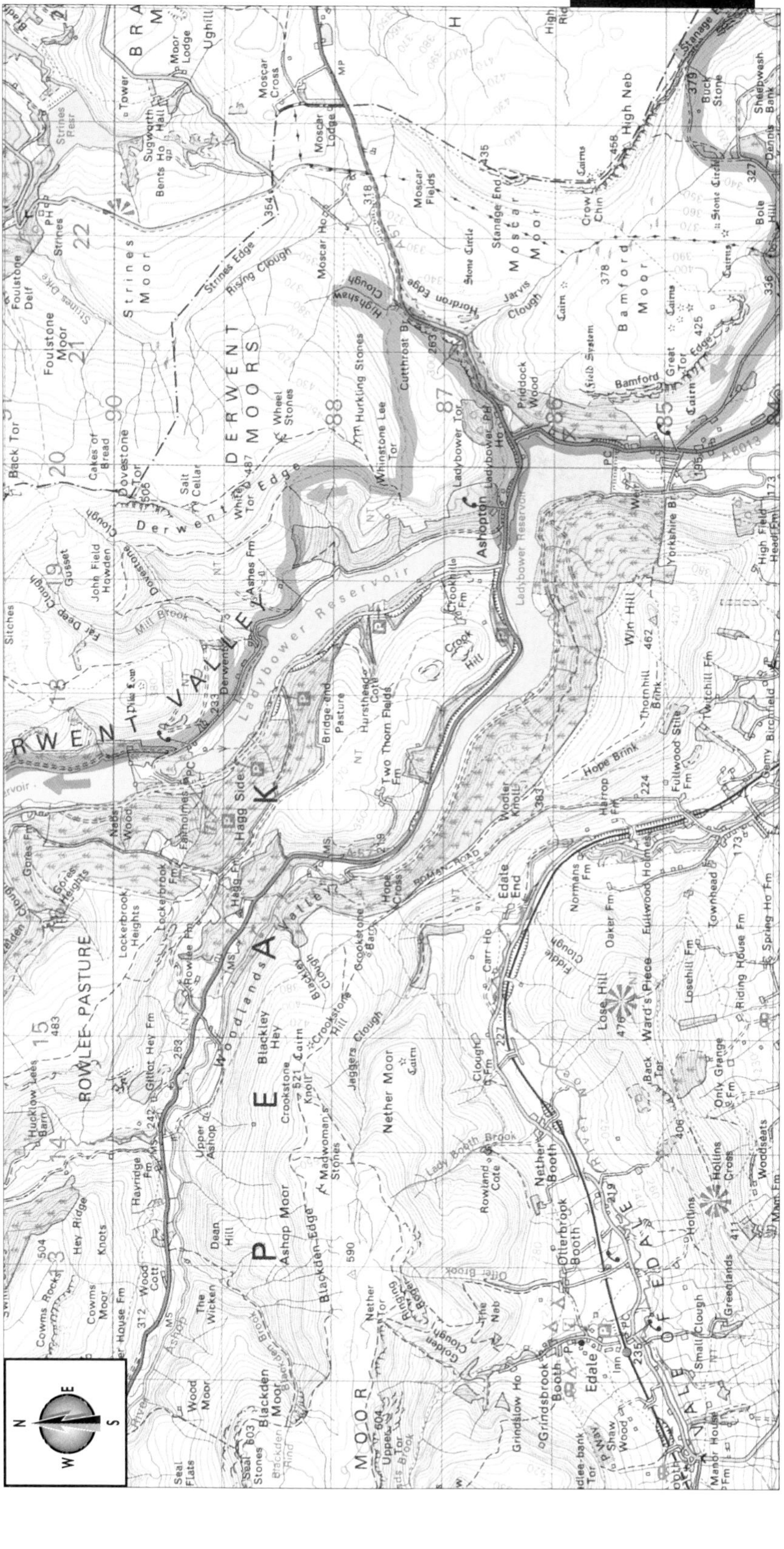

DAY 5 Maps 8 – 10

HATHERSAGE TO LANGSETT (YHA OPEN W/Es ONLY)
21 miles/34km (16m/26km off-road)
2200ft/675m climbing
Summits and Passes: Whinstone Lee 1280ft/390m; Margery Hill 1740ft/530m; Hingcliff Hill 1130ft/345m

After yesterday's epic ride you'll be glad to take it easy. Unless, of course, Langsett YHA is closed. Then I recommend a day's lay-off, give the bikes a good service and give those limbs a holiday before you tackle another long leg – this time to Crowden. If you need any difficult-to-get bike bits there's a good train service into the centre of Sheffield. It's a road spin to Ashopton then it's dial straight into excellent single-tracking. Once again the Peaks put on a spectacular scenic display culminating in the sombre isolation of the Howden Moors and then you're into the magnificent descent down Mickleden Edge, over the Don (the little one) and down in to Langsett.

HATHERSAGE   From YHA turn R (W) on A625 for 1.5m/2.4km to T-junction with A6013 (garage here sells spray lube), and turn R (N) for 3m/4.8km, through Bamford, to A57. (See page 82 for HPT White Loop link to Edale YHA.) Turn L (WSW) (towards Manchester) for 0.5m/0.8km to take hairpin turn R (NW then E), just before bridge, up tarmac bridleway at first for 0.25m/0.4km, through Ashopton, to join single-track after second gate. SO (E) for 1.5m/2.4km on roller coaster bridleway, crossing rocky ford, to lip of Highshaw Clough.

HIGHSHAW   Here bridleway swings L (N then W) to climb for
CLOUGH   1m/1.6km to col at Whinstone Lee Tor (viewpoint!), then swing R (N) for 0.75m/1.2km on contouring bridleway to T-junction then turn L (W) for 0.9m/1.4km on obvious single-track (steep and/or rubbly at times), between two barns, down to gated track.

UPPER   Turn R (NW) alongside Ladybower Reservoir for
DERWENT   1.2m/1.9km, joining tarmac at Derwent, to fork R
VALLEY   (N) for 1.75m/2.8km on gated bridleway to fork

MAP 10

then keep L (NNE) for 1.7m/2.7km, passing Howden Dam and parallelling shoreline, to fork then keep R (NE) for 1.1m/1.75km to cross wooden footbridge.

Turn R (NE) for 110yds/100mts to then fork R (ENE then ESE) on single-track bridleway for 0.3m/0.5km up Cranberry Clough and climb to top of steep spur (bike carry).

Swing L (NE then E then NE) for 0.9m/1.4km up peaty single-track to cairn 550yds/500m NW of Margery Hill trig. Go SO (NE then NNE) for 1.3m/2.1km along Cut Gate to head of Mickleden Beck valley then go SO (N) along E side of valley for 2.4m/3.8km on obvious single-track bridleway, keeping SO (N) at T-junction with waymarker and again SO (N) at bridleway T-junction after going over Hingcliff Hill, down swichbacks to Little Don Bridge. Cross over and go SO (N) for 0.25m/0.4km, up steep climb then swing L (N), to T-junction with waymarker.

For Langsett YHA swing R (E) (Note: you will return on this route to rejoin the HPT so memorise it as you go.) for 0.12m/0.2km to A616 (car park here) then turn R (SE) for 1m/1.6km to Langsett. **(Suggested overnight stop but W/Es only. You should book in advance and it's a self-catering hostel)**

OFF-ROAD CODE

● **Keep to Public Rights of Way across farmland**

● **Use gates and stiles to cross boundaries**

● **Leave livestock, crops and machinery alone**

● **Take your litter home**

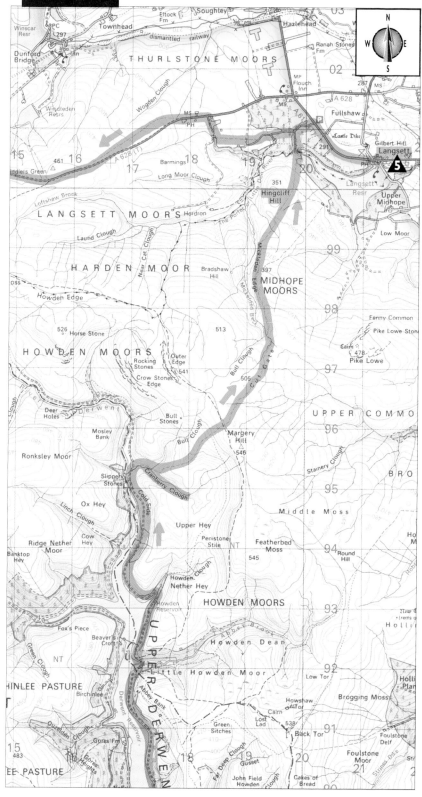

MAP 10

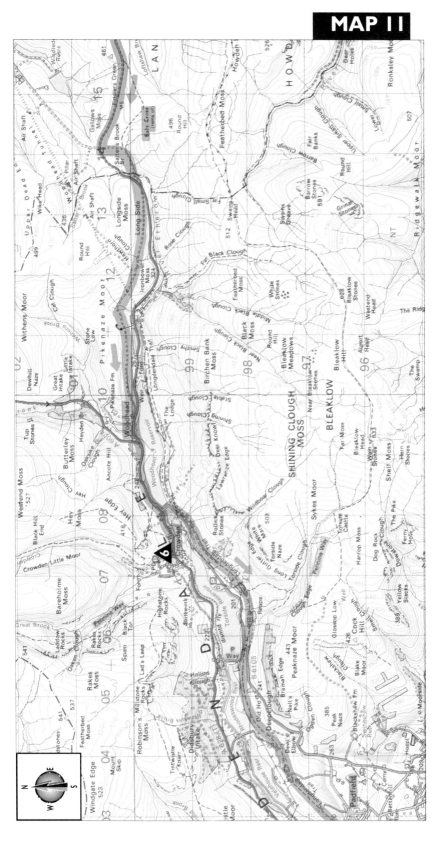

MAP 11

DAY 6 Maps 10 – 11

LANGSETT TO CROWDEN
10 miles/16km (7m/11km off-road)
750ft/230m climbing
Summits and Passes: Lady's Cross 1545ft/470m

If you're feeling really fit and the machines need no maintenance then you could complete the loop today; otherwise take the short hop to Crowden and use the spare time for some well-earned R&R. Navigation is simple, the cycling less extreme in every sense and there's a long descent into Longdendale.

LANGSETT
To continue the HPT hairpin turn L (WSW) for 0.25m/0.4km to T-junction then zig-zag L/R (effectively SO) (W) for 0.12m/0.2km to T-junction then turn R (W) through gate for 0.5m/0.8km through another gate then fork R (NNW) for 0.25m/0.4km to A628 (very busy road).

SALTER'S BROOK BRIDGE
Turn L (W) for 0.3m/0.5km to fork R (W) just after pub on grassy bridleway track for 1.3m/2.1km to rejoin A628 for 1.5m/2.2km to X-roads with C-road and bridleway then turn L (S then WSW) for 0.75m/1.2km, over Salter's Brook bridge, to staggered X-roads with A628 and there zig-zag L/R (effectively SO) (W) for 2.5m/4km on bridleway track down N side of Longdendale valley to rejoin A628 at Woodhead.

Turn R (W) for 1.5m/2.4km (after for 0.75m/1.2km you can fork R onto parallel bridleway for 0.4m/0.65km before rejoining the A628), passing T-junction with B6105, to

 Crowden YHA **(Suggested overnight stop)**.

OFF-ROAD CODE
● **Do not contaminate water**
● **Protect wild flora and fauna**

Burbage Moor marks an end to a long stretch of tarmac and the start of some superb off-roading.

DAY 7 Maps 11 – 12 [*refer to Map 1 for the finish]

CROWDEN TO EDALE
23 miles/37km (12m/19km off-road)
3000ft/925m climbing
Summits and Passes: Monks Road 1245ft/379m;
Lantern Pike 1115ft/340m; Edale Cross 1775ft/541m

It's just as well that the Longdendale Trail gives the legs time to loosen up because hauling yourself out of Glossop is hard work. Once it's done the loop round Lantern Pike provides some entertaining rut and rock hopping then it's a plunge down to Hayfield (ideal spot for a cuppa) before the long, hard ascent to Edale Cross – the highest point on the ride. For a fitting finale the High Peak Trail slips over the edge of Edale Head on Jacob's Ladder – a legendary descent that's demonic when wet, still dicey when dry! Then you're home free!

CROWDEN 'THE LONGDEN-DALE TRAIL RAIL-PATH'
Return 0.4m/0.65km to turn R (SE) for 150yds/140mts on B6105, crossing Woodhead Dam, to 'The Longdendale Trail rail-path' access point then turn R (SW) for 4.4m/7km, executing a zig-zag R/L (effectively SO) (W) to cross the B6105, to C-road in Padfield. Turn R (WNW then SW) away from bridge for 0.12m/0.2km to T-junction and fork L (WSW) for 140yds/125mts, past station, to X-roads. Fork L (SSW) (effectively SO, keeping chapel on your R), for 1m/1.6km down to A57 in Dinting Vale then turn L (SE) for 0.75m/1.2km to roundabout.

CHARLES-WORTH
Turn R (SSW) on 2nd exit (towards Simmondley and Charlesworth) for 1.5m/2.4km to T-junction at Charlesworth then turn L (S then SSW) for 1.7m/2.7km, over Slack Edge, to Plainsteads T-junction.

MATLEY MOOR
Turn R (W) then lane swings L (S) for 0.4m/0.65km to R bend then go SO (S) on single-track bridleway for 0.25m/0.4km, over Matley Moor and over awkward stile, to gated track then turn L (SSE) for 0.8m/1.3km, swing R (SSE) by Matleymoor Farm, to gated bridleway/footpath X-roads with waymarker Go SO (SSE) (towards Birch Vale) for 1.1m/1.75km, across field and

MAP 12

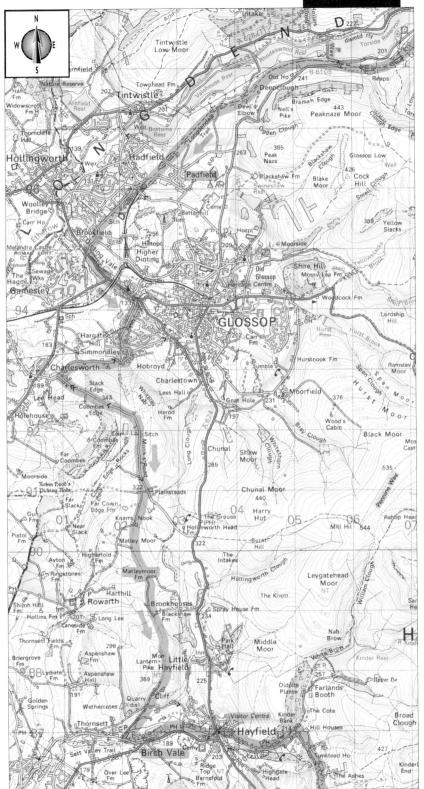

through gate then to keep L (SSE) after short climb, to staggered X-roads with C-road then zig-zag R/L (effectively SO), (SW) for 0.2m//0.3km to gated T-junction.

BIRCH VALE Go SO (SW) through gate for 0.25m/0.4km down track to C-road in Birch Vale then turn L (ESE) for 0.12m/0.2km to turn L (NE then E) through gate onto Sett Valley Trail for 1m/1.6km to car park in Hayfield. Use underpass to cross A624 (walk), passing by church into village centre (café opposite). Turn L (N) for 80yds/75mts then fork R (NE then SE) up Bank Street for 0.8m/1.3km, past pub, then then turn R (SE) over bridge then lane zig-zags L/R (NE then SE) for 0.5m/0.8km, over another bridge, to fork. Keep R (SSE) for 0.25m/0.4km, up through gate, to 2nd fork then keep L (SSE) for 0.5m/0.8km, past Coldwell Clough farm, to T-junction.

EDALE CROSS Go SO (E then ENE) for 1.3m/2.1km to gate at Edale Cross. (Highest point on the route; it's downhill from here on – nearly.) Go SO (E) for 0.7m/1.15km (steep descent; first paved section treacherous when wet) to bridleway/footpath T-junction then turn R (S then NNE) for

JACOB'S LADDER 0.3m/0.5km, through Jacob's Ladder hairpin, to packhorse bridge. Cross bridge and go SO (ESE) on gated track then C-road for 2m/3.2km to familiar T-junction in Edale. Still buzzing from dropping down Jacob's Ladder?

Turn L (N then ENE) for 2.2m/3.5km ride back to Edale YHA where you can raise a glass in honour

of your cycling prowess. **(Suggested overnight stop)**

OFF-ROAD CODE
- **Take special care on country roads**
- **Make no unnecessary noise**

MAP 13

HPT WHITE LOOP
Homeward bound link to Edale YHA from A57/A6013 T-junction, Ladybower
Distance: (8 miles/13km)

ASHOPTON

Turn L (WSW) (towards Manchester), for 0.8m/1.3km, over bridge, to T-junction and turn R (N) for 1.5m/2.4km to T-junction with bridleway track by car park. Turn L (WSW) for 0.7m/1.15km up bridleway to gated T-junction then turn R (NW) for 0.6m/1km, alongside forest, to X-roads then turn L (S) for 0.5m/0.8km (steep

HAGG FARM

switchbacks!), briefly joining Hagg Farm drive, to staggered X-roads with A57 then zig-zag L/R (effectively SO), (S) for 0.1m/0.15km (steep and slippery when wet) to cross bridge. Turn L (SE) for 1m/1.6km on bridleway track, which soon swings R for rocky push up through forest, to

HOPE CROSS

bridleway X-roads near Hope Cross. Go SO (SW) for 1.5m/2.4km, through Jaggers Clough (steep, rutted descent!) on obvious track passing N of Clough Farm, to C-road in Edale.

Turn R(SW) for 0.3m/0.5km to complete the White Loop at Edale YHA. Well done!

OFF-ROAD CODE
- Cycle only on permitted **Rights of Way**
- Give way to horse riders and walkers
- Do not ride in such a manner that you are a danger to others

MAP 13

HPT DARK LOOP
Outward bound link to Ashopton, Ladybower

Distance: (10 miles/16km)

EDALE YHA Start at Edale YHA entrance (GR140861) and turn L (E) for 2.6m/4.2km, under railway, to pick up county unclassified road off L (NNE) just before bridge over Noe. Climb for 2.4m/3.8km, past farm entrance and on to join gated track, to bridleway X-roads just beyond Hope Cross then turn R for 1.1m/1.75km, down through steep R/L/R/L zig-zags (boulder-strewn – beware!) in forest, over bridge and on up to A57.

HAGG FARM Zig-zag L/R (effectively SO) 100yds/100mts up Hagg Farm drive then keep R (N) up switchback bridleway track for 0.4m/0.65km to bridleway X-roads.

BRIDGE-END PASTURE Turn R (SE) for 1.5m/2.4km, SO at bridleway T-junction and over Bridge-End Pasture, to field gate after grass descent. Swing L (ESE then SSE) for 1m/1.6km, following guide posts to track, to pick up Crookhill Farm drive down to C-road.

DARK LOOP LINKS WITH ASHOPTON Turn R (S) for 0.5m/0.8km to A57 then turn L for 0.25m/0.4km, over bridge, to pick up HPT at Ashopton. (See page 72.)

OFF-ROAD CODE
- Do not race
- Keep erosion to a minimum and do not skid
- Be courteous and considerate to others

MAP 13

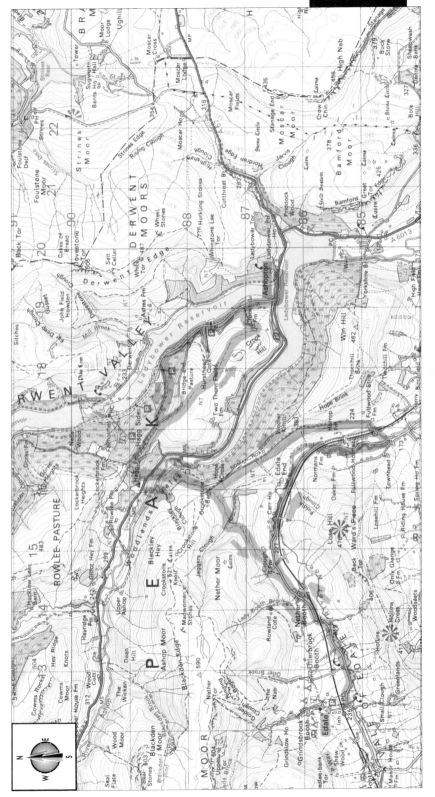

DAY RIDES ON THE HIGH PEAK TRAILS

The following three-day rides are all circular tours which can either be added to the main route, or completed as separate tours in themselves. The maps for these day rides follow in the next few pages.

Ladybower Loops [Map A]

Distance: 18m/29km (13m/21km off-road)
Time: 3 hours
A triple loop that demands peak performance against a backdrop of impressive panoramas over ridge and reservoir. Not a ride for the technically challenged – though I did meet a 'first-timer' tackling the Hagg Farm descent once – it packs in some tricky dips plus a few, fast-track descents with a dash of rubble to boost the adrenalin buzz. Can be ridden in almost every way that these three loops can be strung together.

LOCATION

ROUTE DIRECTIONS

DERWENT RESERVOIR

Start National Park Information Centre car park (GR173893). Turn R (NNE) for 1.25m/2km, along W side of Derwent Reservoir, to fork L (SSW then SE) for 1.5m/2.4km, up through forest then past Lockerbrook Farm, to bridleway X-roads above Hagg Farm. Go SO (S) for 0.5m/0.8km (steep switch-backs!), briefly joining Hagg Farm drive, to staggered X-roads with A57 then zig-zag L/R (effectively SO) (S) for 0.1m/0.15km (steep and slippery when wet) to cross bridge. Turn L (SE) for 1m/1.6km on bridleway track, which soon swings R for rocky push up through forest, to bridleway X-roads near Hope Cross. Go SO (SW) for 1.5m/2.4km, through Jaggers Clough (steep, rutted descent!) on obvious track passing N of Clough Farm, to C-road in Edale. Turn L (ENE) for 2.3m/3.7km, under railway, to pick up county unclassified road off L (NNE) just before bridge

HOPE CROSS

RIVER NOE over Noe. Climb for 2.4m/3.8km, past farm entrance and on to join gated track, to familiar bridleway cross roads just beyond Hope Cross then SO (NNW) 1.5m/2.4km to track T-junction. Hairpin turn R 0.4m/0.6km to A57 then zig-zag R/L (effectively SO) 1m/1.6km up to familiar bridleway cross roads to go SO (SE) for 1.5m/2.4km, SO at bridleway T-junction and over Bridge-End Pasture, to field gate after grass descent.

CROOKHILL FARM Swing L (ESE then SSE) for 1m/1.6km, following guide posts to track, to pick up Crookhill Farm drive down to C-road. Turn R (S) for 0.5m/0.8km to A57 then turn L for 0.25m/0.4km, over bridge, turn L (NW then N) on gated bridleway track for 4.5m/7.2km, along E side of Ladybower Reservoir, back to T-junction by Information Centre car park.

High Peak Intro Stomp

[MAP B]
Distance: 18m/29km (12m/19km off-road)
Time: 3 hours
If you like a rich, off-road mix of calf-singeing climbs, twisting technical descents, gritty gritstone steps and slick, limestone single-track then you'll love this loop. It's an ideal sampler of what the High Peak Trail proper is all about. Get down to Edale and enjoy. Best ridden anti-clockwise, though it's just as easy to start in Castleton as in Edale.

VALE OF EDALE Start Edale car-parks (GR125853 & GR123853) (security can be a problem – lock your car!) and, from T-junction, head WSW for 1.1m/1.8km over River Noe, to pick up gated bridleway track off R (SW).

CHAPEL GATE Climb for 1.5m/2.4km up Chapel Gate Track (seriously steep in places), swinging L (S) over spur, to bridleway T-junction then turn R (WSW) for 0.5m/0.8km down sunken track to A625. Turn R (WSW) for 0.1m/0.15km to T-junction, turn L (SSE) for 1m/1.6km, past Whitelee, then turn L (E) for 1m/1.6km to T-junction with bridleway track just past Eldon Hill quarry.

ELDON HILL QUARRY

MAP A

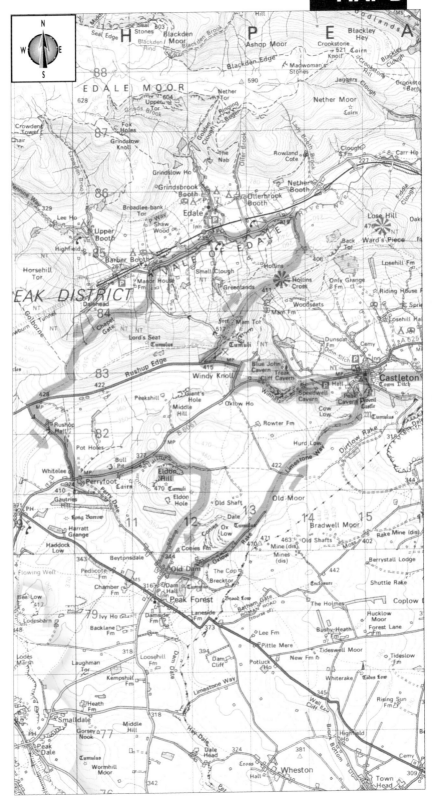

Fork R (E) (heavy plant crossing – take care!) for 0.7m/1.15m, just past humengous hole, then turn R (S) 25yds/25mts, through gate, and continue for 1.25m/2km on bridleway over spur to execute a very lazy R/L to gated track down to T-junction with road.

OLD DAM X ROADS Turn L (SE) for 0.12m/0.2km to Old Dam X-roads and there fork L (E) for 0.3m/0.5km then turn L (NNE) on bridleway drive for 0.1m/0.15km to track T-junction. Turn R (ENE) following obvious

OXLOW RAKE gated track for 1m/1.6km, along Oxlow Rake, to bridleway T-junction by a gate. Keep L (N then NNE) for 0.5m/0.8km to track X-roads N of quarry. Go SO then swing R (NE) along Limestone Way for 0.25m/0.4km to path T-junction in valley bottom then turn R (E), through metal gate, for 1.25m/2km down Cave Dale to T-junction in Castleton. Turn L (W) for 0.1m/0.15km, swinging almost immediately R (N), to T-junction on A625 then turn L (W) for 0.5m/0.8km to T-junction then L for 1.25m/2km up famous

WINNATS PASS Winnats Pass road climb to T-junction then turn R (N) on B6061 for 0.25m/0.4km to T-junction with A625.

MAM TOR Turn L (W) for 0.5m/0.8km to T-junction, turn R (NE) for 0.4m/0.6km, over Mam Tor col, to pick up gated bridleway and fork R (NNE) for 1.1m/1.8km to Hollins Cross. Fork L (N then NE), keeping L of the obvious gully at first, for 1m/1.6km down bridleway single-track, track then farm drive to T-junction. Turn L (W) for 1m/1.6km to start.

OFF-ROAD CODE
- **Be self-sufficient and make sure your bike is safe to ride**
- **Wear a helmet**

MAP C

Big Macc Ramble [MAP C]

Distance: 15m/24km (10m/16km off-road)
Time : 2.5 hours
The North West Water people have generously
provided new permissive cycle-routes within the pine
plantations of Macclesfield Forest. Their tracks are a vital link in
this loop with some of the finest off-road descents in the National
Park culminating in a canter down the shattered remains of the
unclassified road in Cumberland Clough. Best ridden clockwise.

MACCLES-FIELD FOREST CAR PARK AND PICNIC SITE	Start Macclesfield Forest car park and picnic site (GR961711) and turn L (W) out of the car park 0.12m/0.2km then keep R (NNW) at the T-junction 0.5m/0.8km to another T-junction then turn L (WSW) again 0.6m/1km to T-junction in Langley.
LANGLEY	Turn R (NE) 0.7m/1.15km, joining track, to T-junction with bridleway then turn L (NNW) 0.25m/0.4km, over stream, and up to T-junction with unclassified road by Clough House farm. Fork L (N) 0.8m/1.3km, on tarmac lane that crosses to E side of valley, up to A537 at Walker Barn then turn R (E) 140yds/125mts to T-junction and turn R (SSE) again 0.6m/1km.
MACCLES-FIELD FOREST	Just after R bend turn L (ESE) 1m/1.6km on track to Macclesfield Forest hamlet then turn L (NE) then fork R (E) immediately after chapel 0.4m/0.65km down steep track to C-road. Turn L (NE) 0.2m/0.3km, SO (NE) at T-junction, to T-junction in Bottom-of-the-Oven then turn R (ENE) 1m/1.6km up to A537 and fork R (SE)
'CAT AND FIDDLE' PUBLIC HOUSE	0.7m/1.15km to the 'Cat and Fiddle' pub where you turn R (S) onto bridleway 1.5m/2.4km to the A54. Turn R (SW) 0.7m/1.15km to gated unclassified road then turn R (WNW) 1.3m/2.1km, to turn L (W) at T-junction after ford, down past Cumberland Cottage and swinging L (W) over Cumberland Brook, to C-road. Turn R (NNW) 1.1m/1.8km, SO (N) at T-junction soon after, to T-junction and then turn L (WNW) 0.25m/0.4km up to X-roads with gated track. This is the beginning of the NWW cycle-

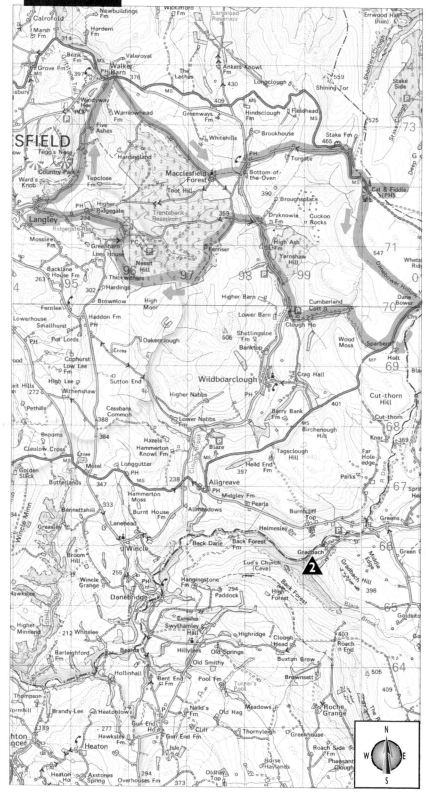

MAP C

NESSIT HILL

route through Macclesfield Forest via Ferriser so please follow their waymarkers. These may differ from the route described. Turn L (S) through gate then 1m/1.6km, through Ferriser's abandoned farm, to track T-junction then turn L (W) 1.2m/1.9km, over Nessit Hill, to gate onto C-road then turn R (E) 0.4m/0.6km, to turn R (E) at next T-junction, to start.

 OFF-ROAD CODE
- **Follow a route marked on a map**
- **Follow the Country Code**

From here Winnats Pass looks an easy climb but wait until you round the corner!

APPENDICES

The following pages are a directory of useful contacts for the High Peak Trail off-road cyclist including YHAs, bike shops, National Park, National Trust, Local Authority and Association offices.

Weather News
Peak District in detail
☎ 01629 813227 (Normal rates)
☎ 04133 670207 (Normal rates)
Peak District Weatherline
☎ 0891 500417

Youth Hostels
Association YHA,
Trevelyan House,
8 St Stephen's Hill,
St Albans, Herts AL1 2DY.
☎ 0727 855215
YHA North England Region for
Camping Barn information
☎ 0629 824571
Youth Hostels en-route
Edale Activity Centre
☎ 01433 670302
Buxton
☎ 01298 22287
Gradbach Mill
☎: 01260 227625
Elton
☎ 01629 650394
Youlgreave
☎ 01629 636518
Hathersage
☎ 01433 650493
Langsett (W/Es only)
☎ 01629 825850

(For bookings
☎ 01742 884541)
Crowden
☎ 01457 852135

Bike Shops
Open Country
3 Market Street
Whaley Bridge
☎ 01663 735020
Stanley Fearn & Son
19 Bakewell Road
Matlock
☎ 01629 582089
J E James Cycles
347-361 Bramall Lane
Sheffield
☎ 01742 550557
Freewheel
140-142 West Street
Sheffield
☎ 01742 569544
Allens Cycles
23 Barnsley Road
Wombwell, Barnsley
☎ 01226 756281
Cyclosport
25 Doncaster Road
Barnsley
☎ 01266 204020

93

British Rail Booking Information

Manchester
☎ 0161 8328353
Sheffield
☎ 01742 726411

Tourist Information Centres

Buxton
☎ 01298 25106
Stafford
☎ 01785 40204
Sheffield
☎ 01742 734671
☎ 01742 795901
Macclesfield
☎ 01625 504114

National Park Offices

Peak National Park Office,
Aldern House, Baslow Road,
Bakewell, Derbyshire DE45 1AE.
☎ 01629 814321

National Trust

East Midlands Regional Office,
Clumber Park Stableyard,
Worksop, Notts S80 3BE.
☎ 01909 486411

County Council Offices (Rights of Way)

County Planning & Highways,
Derbyshire County Council,
Matlock, Derbyshire DE4 3AG.
☎ 01629 580000
Planning Economic
Development, Staffordshire
County Council, Martin Street,
Stafford ST16 2LE.
☎ 01785 223121
Public Rights of Way Unit,
Cheshire County Council,
Commerce House, Hunter Street,
Chester CH1 2QP.
☎ 01244 603563
Rights of Way Officer, Sheffield
☎ 01742 726444
Rights of Way Officer, Barnsley
☎ 01226 770770

North West Water Authority

Recreation & Conservation Dept
☎ 014578 64187

The Cyclists Touring Club

Since 1878 the Cyclists Touring
Club (CTC) has been the
governing body for recreational
cycling in this country and is
recognised by such organisations as
the Sports Council, the
Department of Transport and the
Department of the Environment.
Membership is open to anyone
interested in cycling. They
currently have 40,000 members,
200 nationwide clubs and 100
local clubs affiliated to them.

Recently the CTC has taken on
responsibility for addressing off-
road cycling access issues which
includes promoting Rights of
Way initiatives wherever they
occur and representing the views

of mountain bikers at a local and national levels. Local representation is done through a network of volunteer Access Officers. Those responsible for areas relevant to this ride can be contacted through the main office. Please remember that they are volunteers and carry out their CTC duties without payment and in addition to their normal employment, so please contact them only if there is genuine need.

If you would like to apply for membership then please apply to:

CTC, Dept CSB/94, 69 Meadrow, Godalming, Surrey GU7 3HS.
☎ **0483 417217**

Benefits of being a member include: representation on Rights of Way and access issues in your area. Third Party insurance cover. Free legal advice for cycling related problems. Free legal aid. Free technical advice. Free international touring info. Bi-monthly colour magazine. Free handbook. Mail order service. A voice in the world of MTBing.

AUTHOR'S ACKNOWLEDGEMENTS

For their help in compiling the route and their invaluable advices: Richard Foot, Stuart Gascoigne of Open Country in Whaley Bridge together with The Peak National Park Authority and in particular Paul Hopkins, North West Water Recreation & Conservation – in particular George Grimes – plus the Rights of Way and Highways people in Cheshire, Staffordshire, Derbyshire, Sheffield and Barnsley.

For back-up, advice and technical support: Madison (Shimano); Patrick Adams of Nutriwest; John Mullett of Ralph Coleman Cycles, Taunton, Somerset (01823 275822) and Chris Marley.

For clothing and carrying kit: Polaris MTB wear, North Wave mountain bike boots, Giro helmets, Sub-Zero base-layer clothing and Karrimor rucksacks.

Finally, for supplying hardware: Timax MTB frames, Shocktech suspension forks, Halson suspension forks, Simplon Ti, Michelin tyres and Avocet Vertec computers.